THE DIG

Archaeological Survey of Canada	Commission archéologique du Canada
National Museum of Man	Musée national de l'Homme
National Museums of Canada	Musées nationaux du Canada
Board of Trustees	Conseil d'Administration
National Museums of Canada	Musées nationaux du Canada

Mr. George Ignatieff	Chairman
M. André Bachand	Vice-Président
Dr. W.E. Beckel	Member
M. Jean des Gagniers	Membre
Mr. R.H. Kroft	Member
Mme. Marie-Paule LaBréque	Membre
Mr. J.R. Longstaffe	Member
M. Charles Lussier	Membre
Mr. Gower Markle	Member
Dr. B. Margaret Meagher	Member
Dr. William Schneider	Member
M. Léon Simard	Membre
Mme. Marie Tellier	Membre
Dr. Sally Weaver	Member

Secretary General	Secrétaire Général
National Museums of Canada	Musées nationaux du Canada

Mr. Bernard Ostry

Director	Directeur
National Museum of Man	Musée national de l'Homme

Dr. William E. Taylor Jr.

Chief	Chef
Archaeological Survey of Canada	Commission archéologique du Canada

Dr. George F. MacDonald

Publication supported by	Ouvrage subventionné par
The Margaret Hess	Le Fonds Margaret Hess
Canadian Studies Fund	d'Études canadiennes
of the National Museum of Man	du Musée national de l'Homme

THE DIG

an archaeological reconstruction of a west coast village

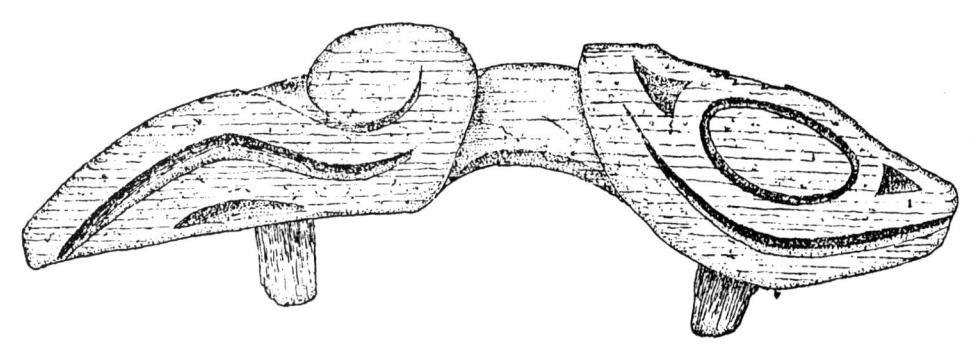

George F. MacDonald
Richard I. Inglis
OTTAWA 1976

ISBN 0-660-00007-5

archaeological survey of Canada
**NATIONAL MUSEUM OF MAN
NATIONAL MUSEUMS OF CANADA**

commission archéologique du Canada
**MUSÉE NATIONAL DE L'HOMME
MUSÉES NATIONAUX DU CANADA**

Cover: View of "The Dig" in the Canada Before Cartier Hall, Victoria Memorial Museum Building, National Museum of Man, National Museums of Canada

Half-Title Page: Motif from a bone piece of personal adornment depicting a recurring series of devouring mouth forms, an important element in Northwest Coast art.

Title page: Carved red cedar handle. Earliest example of a wood art piece from Prince Rupert, B.C. (circa A.D. 320)

© Crown Copyrights reserved

Available by mail from
National Museums of Canada
Marketing Services
Ottawa K1A 0M8

Catalogue No. NMM 92-52/1976

National Museum of Man
National Museums of Canada
Ottawa, Canada
First quarter, 1976

P0987654321
Y79876

Litho in Canada

contents

List of illustrations — F
Summary — H
Résumé — I

I. archaeology as reconstruction

What Is Archaeology? — 3
Choosing A Site For Reconstruction — 12
How The Reconstruction Was Done — 22

II. interpreting the remains

Who Were The People? — 33
What The Skeletons Show — 34
What Did They Eat? — 42
A Tool For Every Purpose — 51
Personal Adornment and Artistic Expression — 62

III. synthesis of the archaeological interpretation

An Outline of Coast Tsimshian Prehistory — 73
Early (3000 BC–1500 BC) — 74
Middle (1500 BC–AD 500) — 77
Late (AD 500–AD 1830) — 77
The Tsimshian Today — 81

acknowledgements — 85

suggested reading list — 87

list of illustrations

Colour Plates

I.	Archaeologists at work	9
II.	The Boardwalk site	19
III.	Art pieces	65
IV.	Cultural revival among the Tsimshian	83

Black-and-White Plates

1. Nineteenth-century artifact collection — 4
2. Aerial photograph of the Boardwalk site and environs — 6
3. Surveying — 7
4. Stratification of a shell midden — 11
5. Garden Island site — 12
6. Kitkatla village, 1881 — 14
7. Rushton Island campsite — 15
8. Excavation of a waterlogged site — 21
9. Cleaning a basketry fragment — 23
10. House post from Skeena River — 24
11. Panorama of "The Dig" in the National Museum of Man, Ottawa — 26/27
12. Typical features reconstructed in "The Dig" — 29
13. Checking the stratigraphy in the reconstruction — 30
14. Self-image of a warrior — 32
15. An excavated human burial — 36
16. Pathologies of prehistoric Prince Rupert — 37
17. Mandibles showing tooth wear — 38
18. Woman wearing a labret — 39
19. Ritualism as evidenced on human skeletal remains — 40
20. A partially carved tibia — 41
21. Clam flats — 42
22. Collecting chitons — 43
23. & 24. River Fishing — 44
25. & 26. Sea Fishing — 45
27. & 28. The Nass River eulachon fishery — 47

29.	Preparing salmon for the smokehouse	48
30.	Collecting a whale skeleton	49
31.	Digging for roots	50
32.	Fishing utensils	53
33.	Making a dugout canoe	55
34.	Woodworking tools	57
35.	Food storage box	59
36.	Making a cedar bark basket	60
37.	Women's tools	61
38.	An historic Coast Tsimshian house, 1879	63
39.	Rock painting from the Skeena River	68
40.	Prince Rupert petroglyph – "Man who fell from heaven"	69
41.	Bear dance ceremony, nineteenth-century drawing	74
42.	Chief's dance, nineteenth-century drawing	75
43.	Weapons of war	76
44.	Tsimshian warrior, nineteenth-century drawing	77
45.	Fort Simpson, 1873	79
46. & 47.	Metlakatla, 1881	80

Figures

1.	Basket	22
2.	Labret (two views)	39
3.	Points for hunting	58
4.	Bone implements	66
5.	Stone concretion	67
6.	Whalebone club	70
7.	Chronology	72

Maps

1.	Contour map of the Boardwalk site	10
2.	Contour map of the Garden Island site	13
3.	Distribution of prehistoric sites in Prince Rupert harbour area	16
4.	Map of the north coast of British Columbia	34

summary

This book is written for the general public as a guide to "THE DIG", a special feature of the Canada Before Cartier Hall in the National Museum of Man in Ottawa. "THE DIG" is a reconstruction of an actual West Coast archaeological excavation, spanning 5,000 years of history of a Canadian Indian village. It is the story of the Coast Tsimshian people.

Three chapters attempt to acquaint the reader with the scope, objectives and techniques of archaeology; with the interpretation of what is found in an archaeological excavation; and with the prehistory of the Coast Tsimshian villages and people, as revealed by National Museum of Man archaeological projects.

résumé

Ce livre s'adresse au grand public et sert de guide pour LA FOUILLE, une présentation spéciale dans la salle d'archéologie du Musée national de l'Homme, à Ottawa. LA FOUILLE est la réplique d'une fouille archéologique réelle de la côte Ouest qui représente cinq mille années de l'histoire d'un village canadien. C'est l'histoire des Tsimshians de la Côte.

Trois des chapitres cherchent à familiariser le lecteur avec la portée, les objectifs et les techniques de l'archéologie, avec l'interprétation des objets découverts dans une fouille et avec la préhistoire des villages des Tsimshians de la Côte, tels que les révèlent les travaux archéologiques entrepris par le Musée national de l'Homme.

1. archaeology as reconstruction

I. Archaeology as Reconstruction

What is archaeology?

Discoveries of the remains of activities of prehistoric peoples rarely fail to generate excitement and curiosity. One does not have to have a special interest in the past to share such feelings, whether the discovery be of arrowheads turned up in a plowed field, or of the ruins of an ancient civilization. Rather, man's interest in people of other times and places appears as natural as it is intense.

The foundations of archaeology, as an academic discipline, were laid by men whose imaginations were stirred by evidence which hinted at the heretofore unsuspected antiquity of man's presence on this planet, and the complexity of his biological and cultural evolution. Many others were motivated only by the collecting spirit, by a search for priceless art objects, for "lost" civilizations, and for fame and fortune. During the past two hundred years, reports of the findings of these explorers and collectors have been eagerly followed by a public that is still much under the influence of the romantic notions fostered by the Great Age of Exploration.

Yet archaeology is much more than just a romantic undertaking, even though many misconceptions about the discipline are still prevalent in the public mind. Just what it is that archaeologists do – how the raw data for scientific analysis is collected, and how the cultures of past peoples are studied and reconstructed – often may seem mysterious to the non-scientist. In particular, the public has not yet become aware of the nature of the developing field and laboratory methods by which archaeologists excavate and interpret the remains of a prehistoric settlement.

Archaeology involves controlled methods of survey and excavation, aimed at recovering discarded objects and remains which provide information about the structures and activities of people in

Plate 1. During the late nineteenth century, many institutions were eagerly amassing great collections of artifacts from contemporary "primitive" cultures throughout the world, usually with little attention given to the people who actually made and used them. The stone implements above were collected from Port Simpson, British Columbia, for the Berlin Museum (Germany) by an American Naval officer, Ensign A.P. Niblack, in 1885.

the past. The relationships of these objects and remains can be reconstructed, and their cultural meaning determined. Since so much of the material which survives the passage of time consists of tools, weapons, and other implements, archaeologists attach great importance to the technologies of vanished peoples.

The archaeologist uses various terms to describe his finds. Items which were deliberately fashioned by man to serve some purpose, such as tools and ornaments, are called *artifacts,* and the whole collection of artifacts from any given site is called an *assemblage*. Structures, including remains of dwellings, and food-processing and cooking areas, are called *features*. The term, *samples,* refers to controlled collections of bones, seeds, shells, soils, and wood ash.

There are many different kinds of sites – habitation sites, animal kill sites, stone quarry sites and burial ground sites – each requiring particular methods of excavation. In general, however, to record the relationships between artifacts, features and samples, the archaeologist first maps and grids a site, establishing squares of uniform dimensions. He then excavates the deposits within these units in thin layers. Each find is measured in terms of the distance and depth from one or more fixed reference points. For interpretation to be meaningful, the relative locations of the cultural remains are vital.

Stratigraphy is a basic concept of archaeology. Simply, this means that the oldest remains at a site are found at the deepest levels, with the more recent in progressive layers one on top of the other, up to the present-day surface of the ground. Stratification at different sites can vary greatly, further complicating the archaeologist's work. At some sites, natural layering may be lacking, and the deposits may continue down through many feet of the same type of soil. At others, the stratification may be disturbed, either by natural events or by the activities of men. However, whether the archaeologist excavates by following natural stratification or by arbitrary units, he can usually determine the age of an artifact, relative to others at the site, by noting the level from which it came.

The process of dating, especially, depends on pin-pointing the exact spot where an artifact or other bit of evidence is found. The task of establishing a cultural sequence for a given site depends primarily on *relative dating,* which merely indicates that one find is older or younger than another. Dates which are keyed to our modern calendar are termed *absolute*. Methods of dating by the

Plate 2. During the first half of this century, most remains of the activities of prehistoric peoples were discovered accidentally, during farming or land clearing operations. In the past few decades, however, the number of professional archaeologists in Canada has increased from a handful to a hundred, so that nowadays such sites are usually found by carefully conducted surveys. Using maps, aerial photographs, and historical records, the archaeologist determines the factors which made particular locations desirable to prehistoric peoples in a given area, and then systematically checks these potential spots by air and land survey. The sites found are then evaluated and a sample of the most promising ones is selected for excavation.

Aerial photo showing the location of the Boardwalk site in Prince Rupert harbour.

Plate 3. An archaeologist checks elevations to prepare a contour map of a site.

analysis of the physical and/or chemical properties of certain remains, as well as by various other techniques, have been refined over recent decades, and have made both relative and absolute dating somewhat easier. Nevertheless, dating poses many difficult problems for the archaeologist.

This description is necessarily greatly simplified. No comprehensive discussion of all archaeological field techniques — let alone the complex problems of archaeological interpretation and the different theoretical approaches — could be offered here. However, there are some excellent books on archaeology, examples of which have been included in our Suggested Reading List. Most are available from public libraries.

The primary aim behind the reconstruction of an actual excavation at the National Museum of Man in Ottawa was to demonstrate some of the methods and strategies used in field archaeology. In 1969, the Museum closed its doors, in order to make structural renovations to the Victoria Memorial Museum Building, and at the same time new displays were prepared for installation. "The Dig" was one of the first features of the new archaeology gallery to be undertaken. The large number of visitors to the gallery to date indicates the extent of public interest.

Colour Plate I. Archaeologists at work

An abandoned house feature, with a sunken interior pit is being excavated. This structure was lived in as late as 1830. 'Knu site, in the Venn Passage area of Prince Rupert harbour, 1972.

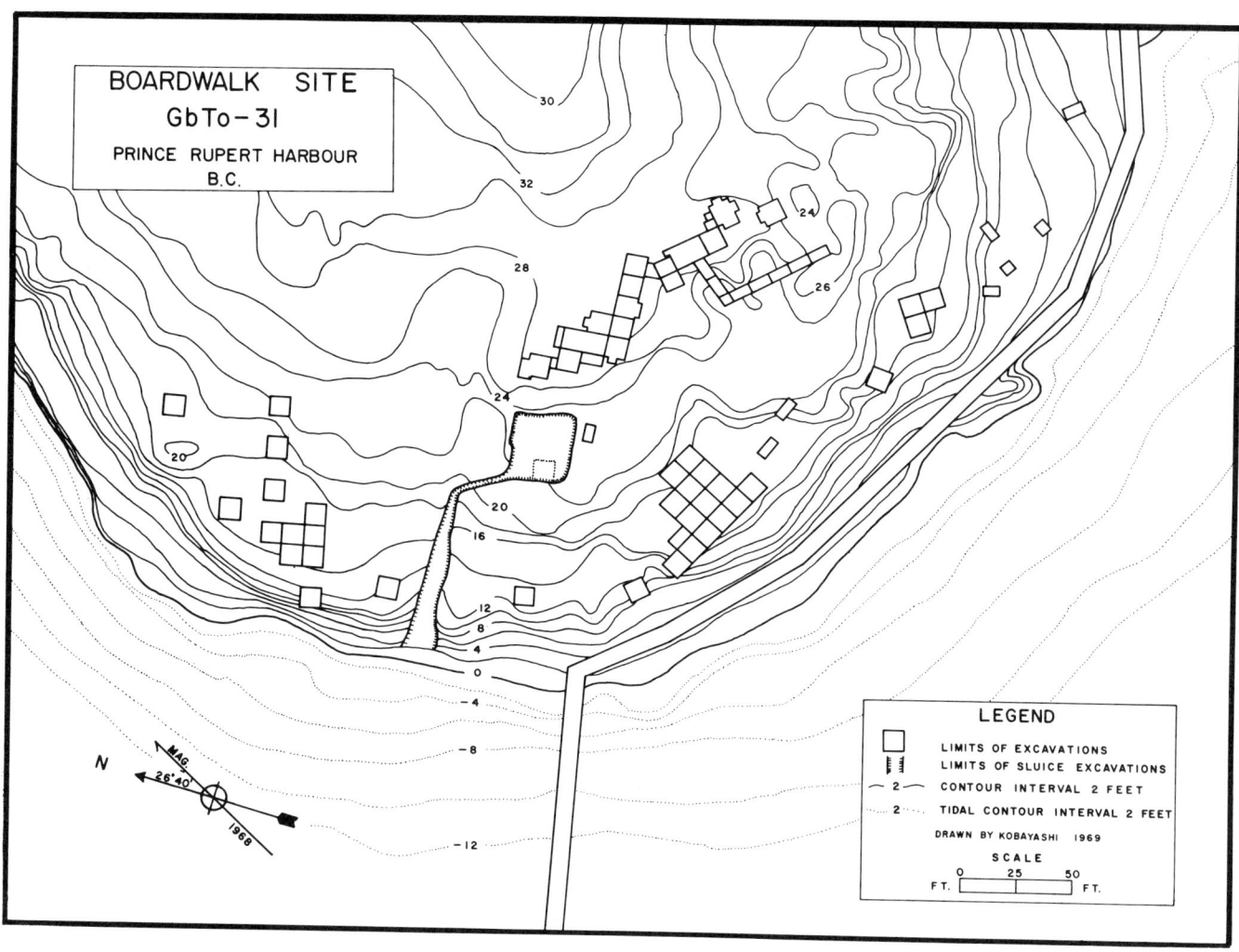

Map 1. Preliminary site maps are made before the excavations begin, and are modified as the work progresses.

Plate 4. Stratification at a typical Northwest Coast midden in the Prince Rupert area consists of layer upon layer of shell refuse. These deposits reached a depth of over 20 feet (6.1 metres). Lachane site, 1973.

Choosing a site for reconstruction

Museum specialists from the Archaeological Survey of Canada wanted to reconstruct portions of a site in Canada where the widest possible range of archaeological problems were encountered. In doing so, it was felt that a person who did not have the benefit of visiting a real dig would be able to see the relationships between artifacts and features, just as the archaeologist found them.

It was necessary to select a site which: (1) had been occupied for a long time, and had deep deposits to demonstrate stratigraphy; (2) had good preservation with a range of materials represented, including bone, wood, shell and stone; (3) had a wide range of features, such as the remains of dwellings, food-processing areas, tool-manufacturing areas, and cemeteries, which would reflect the lifestyle of the occupants.

The northern British Columbia coast, centred around Prince Rupert, is one of the oldest, continuously occupied regions of the New World. It poses some of the most complex problems of archaeological interpretation faced by prehistorians in Canada. In the last ten years, nearly 200 sites have been found along an 800-square-mile (2072-square-kilometre) section of coastline in this region.

Plate 5. Canoe skidways lining a beach led to the discovery of a small village site on Garden Island in Prince Rupert harbour.

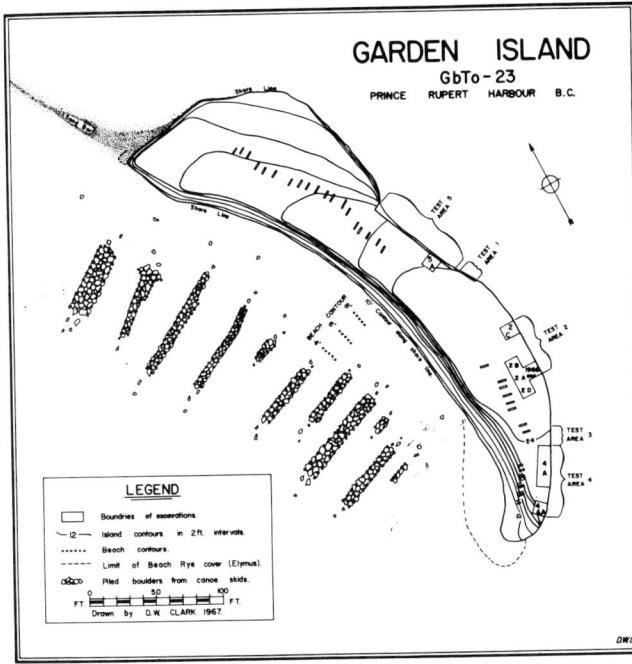

Map 2. Excavations on Garden Island, showing the remains of stone skidways.

Every one of these sites is situated on the narrow coastal plain, usually no more than a few steps from the sea, upon which the people relied so heavily for their livelihood. Village sites are generally near extensive clam flats and just back of an abrupt embankment above the high water mark. Stone skidways, for hauling canoes up the beach, are often the archaeologist's first clues regarding location of a former village. Such sites represent areas of population concentration and well-established residences.

Sites at which food was processed are, naturally, close to areas where there is, or was, an abundance of a particular food species. At such camps on the north Pacific coast, salmon and *eulachon* (candle fish) were dried and smoked, and sea mammals were butchered. Others were near places where seaweed or birds' eggs were gathered. Most of these camps were occupied by few people for short periods of time, and thus, archaeological deposits of this kind are not extensive.

Between 1966 and 1973, 10 of the 50 sites in the immediate area of Prince Rupert harbour were excavated. From these, over 15,000 artifacts, several hundred burials, 200,000 pieces of animal bone, and hundreds of samples of

archaeology as reconstruction **13**

Plate 6. Kitkatla, the oldest continuously occupied village on the Northwest Coast, is the only Coast Tsimshian settlement with traditional poles still standing today. The steep rise of the midden in front of the houses is typical of winter village sites. This photograph was taken by E. Dossetter in 1881.

Plate 7. During the long summer days, a fishing camp on Rushton Island in Hecate Strait bustled with activity. The catch was dried on racks or strung in smoke houses. Structures at food-collecting camps were far less permanent than those of the winter villages. C.F. Newcombe photograph, early 1900s.

archaeology as reconstruction

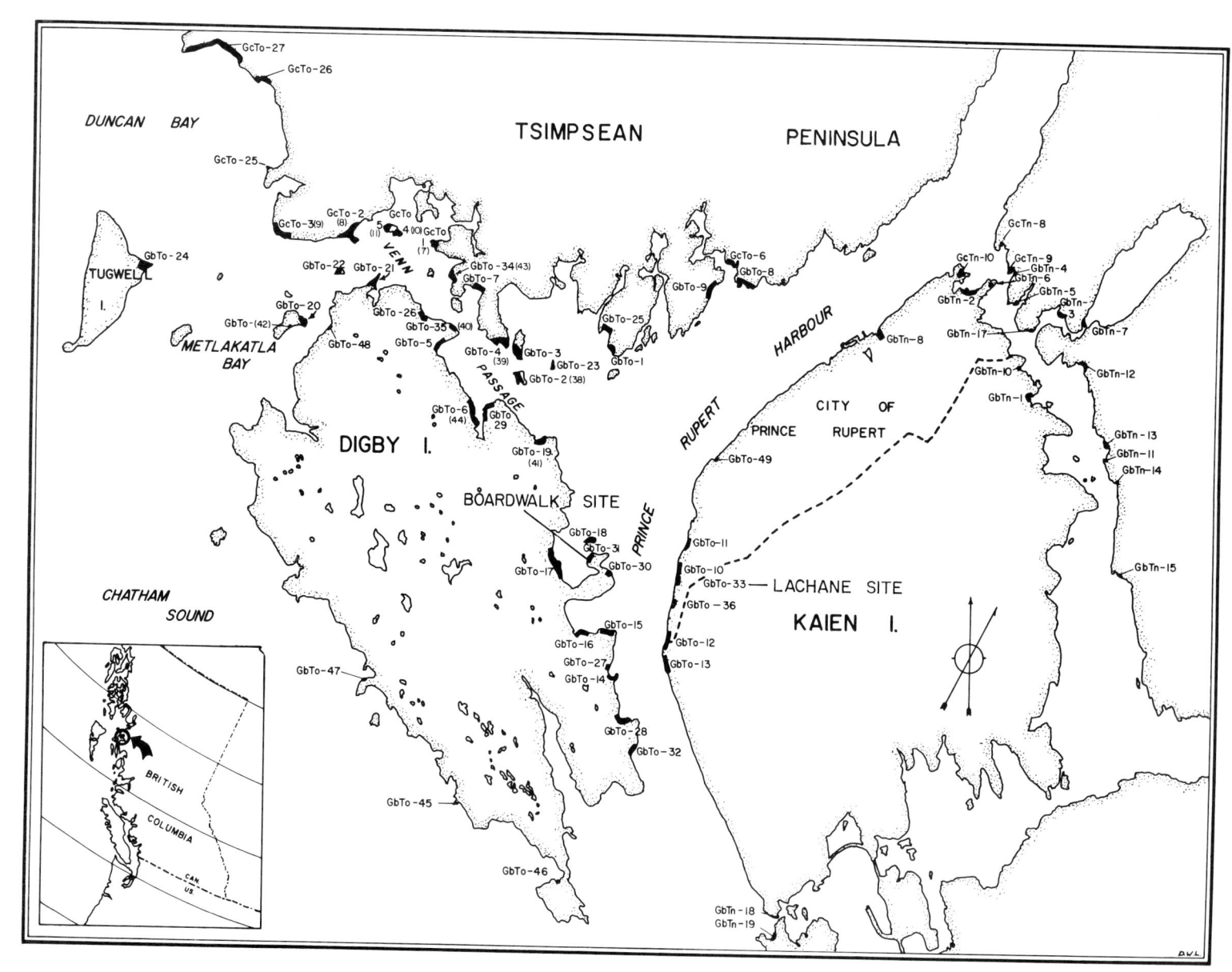

Map 3. The Prince Rupert harbour area. All sites of prehistoric settlement (villages and camps) known to date are indicated. Note that all cluster along the shorelines.

archaeology as reconstruction

soil, shell, and burned wood have been collected. A quarter of a million cubic feet (7,000 cubic metres), of cultural deposit have been examined so far, less than one percent of the total deposit represented by all 50 sites.

Museum archaeologists ultimately chose the Boardwalk site (GbTo 31), in Prince Rupert harbour, as best meeting the requirements of the new gallery. This site, excavated by National Museum of Man crews between 1968 and 1970, was a major winter village of one of the nine tribes of the Coast Tsimshian. It measures 600 feet (182.4 metres), along the shoreline, by 200 feet (60.8 metres), inland, and reaches a depth of 20 feet (6.1 metres). It is estimated to contain half a million cubic feet (14,000 cubic metres) of cultural deposit.

As at many other village sites on the British Columbia coast, the Boardwalk deposits consist mainly of layer upon layer of the shells of clams, cockles, and mussels. Shellfish made up much of the winter diet of the people in this region. Similar "midden" deposits, the garbage dumps of prehistoric settlements, are commonly found in many parts of the world — Scandinavia, the Far East, eastern North America — along sea coasts and estuaries and even far inland along rivers.

The house floors consist of black humus-rich soil and gravel with little or no shell. Within the remains of the dwellings were found small, egg-shaped stones, which were heated and dropped into wooden cooking boxes to boil water. These turned up in large concentrations, along with numbers of bigger rocks used to hold down roof planks and rocks from hearths.

Excellent preservation of bone and antler artifacts is characteristic of shell middens. The shell, basically calcium, is slowly dissolved in the ground by the plentiful rainfall in the region. This produces a chemical solution of calcium carbonate, which neutralizes the acids given off by the roots of living plants. It is the plant acids which destroy bone objects of the remote past in most archaeological sites in Canada. At the Boardwalk site, the soil has preserved bone and antler extremely well, and 3,000 artifacts of this material were recovered, along with 20,000 animal bones.

Other soil conditions sought by the archaeologist are found in those portions of a site which are water-saturated, because of poor drainage. A typical area might be the bed of a sluggish stream into which the former inhabitants of the site discarded things from time to time.

Such water-saturated soils are free from bacterial action that destroys wood and vegetable fibres. At the Boardwalk and Lachane sites some 400 artifacts of wood and basketry were found.

Recovery of these perishable artifacts entails a special technique. Whereas most excavating is done with small trowels, shovels, buckets, and screens for sifting the soil, water-logged deposits are removed with jets of water from high-pressure pumps. The water breaks up and washes away the matrix of thick mud, exposing the fragile materials. By varying the water pressure from a powerful jet to a gentle spray, almost every type of material can be recovered undamaged.

A shell midden presents a wide variety of archaeological problems, as well as great possibilities for recovering valuable evidence of past human activities. Such a deposit is literally taken apart under microscopic scrutiny, since every stone and shell has been placed there by man.

Colour Plate II. Taking its name from the government pier constructed by the Department of Transport, the Boardwalk Site lines some 600 feet (182.4 metres) of shore. Its extensive deposits, reaching inland for 200 feet (60.8 metres), contain an estimated half million cubic feet (14,000 cubic metres), of debris, left during 5,000 years of human occupation.

Inset: Encroaching forest has reclaimed the village sites over the past 200 years. During a survey of the area, archaeologists stumbled on the remains of house structures blanketed by lush undergrowth.

archaeology as reconstruction

Plate 8. Hundreds of artifacts which normally decay rapidly in the ground — wooden bowls and boxes, digging sticks, arrow shafts, basketry, and rope — were recovered from a 2,000-year-old waterlogged deposit at the Lachane site near Prince Rupert. Saturated by an ancient stream bed, the soil in which the perishable remains were preserved had to be carefully washed away with hoses. This site subsequently was destroyed, to make way for a shipping terminal for the harbour.

How the reconstruction was done

Materials needed for the reconstruction were collected during the 1969 and 1970 field seasons of the National Museum's Prince Rupert project, and shipped back to Ottawa in railway boxcars. Twenty tons of shell-bearing deposit were required. Samples of each type of soil had to be sorted and keyed to position in the profiles of the excavation walls. These were then fixed with polyvinyl acetate to suitably sculptured sheets of styrofoam, and assembled to look like the continuous profile of an excavation. Every profile used was an exact copy of one from the Boardwalk site, although some rearranging of features had to be done to fit the space available in the gallery.

To complete the illusion of a real dig, a plantscape was needed. Botanists classified the types of trees and shrubs which grew on the site, and samples of each were gathered and preserved for exhibition. Many techniques had to be developed to preserve the living appearance of the vegetation and, at the same time, meet strict fire code regulations. The limbs of huge cedar trees were preserved intact. Sheets of cedar bark were removed from the trunks and mounted on fibreglass cores at the Museum. Moss, rotted wood, and hemlock,

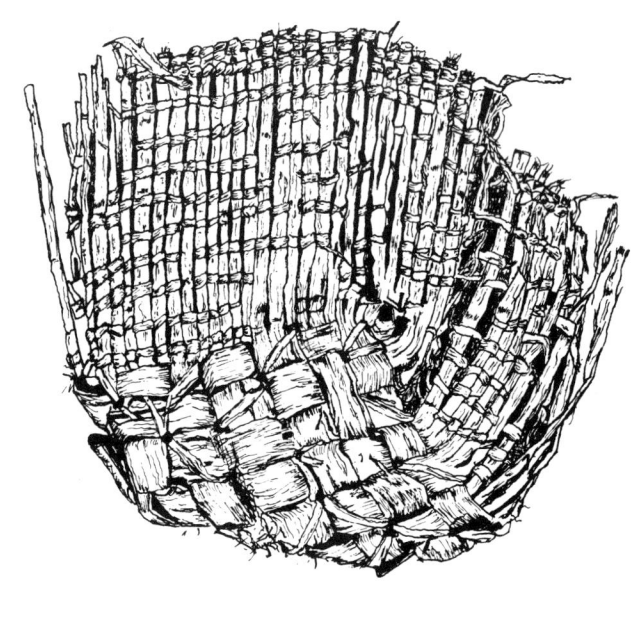

Figure 1. A 2,000-year-old cedar bark basket recovered from the Lachane site. 1/3 actual size.

archaeology as reconstruction

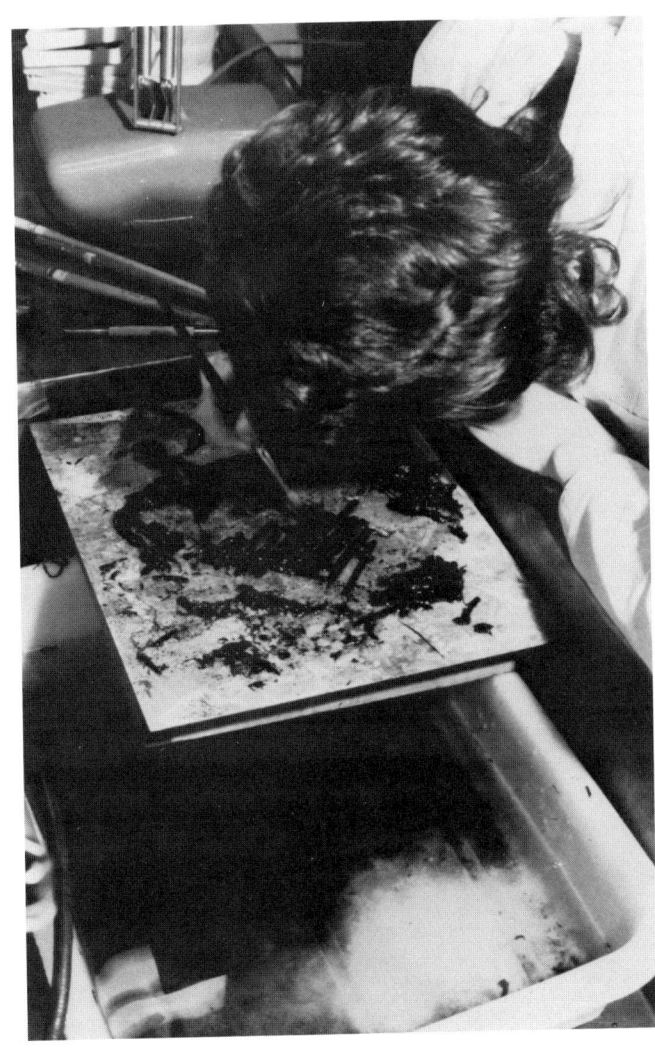

Plate 9. Before artifacts can be catalogued and studied, they must be carefully cleaned. Here, a technician in the National Museum of Man prepares a delicate basketry fragment from a Prince Rupert site.

spruce and fir needles, which were part of the forest floor covering the site, had to be gathered, sorted and fumigated before being taken to the Museum.

The backdrop mural completed the plantscape portion of the dig. The artist used photographs of the actual site, and the result is a rendering in which every feature of the natural habitat in the area is authentic, from every species of tree and plant to an abandoned boat on the beach.

To illustrate the decaying remains of the last occupation of the site, memorial poles and carved house posts were needed. The village at the Boardwalk site was abandoned, prior to contact with Europeans in the 1780's, and no record of these features survived. Fibreglass casts were made of poles from a Skeena River Tsimshian village which had been abandoned in the 1870s, and these were used in the reconstruction.

The artifacts in the reconstructed dig, selected from those actually recovered, are displayed in their exact stratigraphic position. Some rearrangement was required to construct the panels which illustrate the main industries of the villagers. The excavation units in the centre of the gallery are ten-foot (3-metre) squares, gridded with string, the

Plate 10. One of a pair of Skeena River house posts used in the National Museum of Man dig reconstruction. The standing figure is called "Whole-Being". He holds a fish club under his chin. Atop his head the large circular log once supported the roof structure.

same procedure followed in the field when recording finds. Many of the more interesting features have been left on pedestals of earth, as they would have been for recording purposes. These include burials, a rock slab pit with boiling stones and charcoal, and associated artifacts.

A visitor to "The Dig" walks down an inclined ramp, deeper and deeper along the vertical walls of the excavation. It is easy to imagine oneself at a real archaeological dig. Overhead towers the majestic forest canopy of the rainy, temperate Prince Rupert region, and around the excavation is a lush undergrowth of salal bushes and moss. The gallery has the same quiet, cathedral-like quality that the deep forest gloom gives to the actual site. Personal belongings of the excavating crew — raingear, digging tools, a can of bug repellent — lie about amid the shell heaps and bones, reinforcing the feeling that one has entered upon an excavation in progress, perhaps momentarily interrupted by a call to lunch.

Here are revealed 5,000 years of Canadian prehistory. And, here also are revealed those mysterious techniques by which the archaeologists so carefully — so patiently — recover and record the life of a once vital community.

Plate 11. **The Dig**

26 *archaeology as reconstruction*

Plate 12. A selection of features, appearing as they did to the archaeologist in the field, are displayed in this portion of the National Museum of Man's reconstruction of the Boardwalk site. Two adults, buried 800 to 1,200 years ago (a), lay near a cache of warrior's grave goods (b), including a carved whalebone club (page 70), a stone club, a stone dagger, and copper bracelets. At other levels, the complete skeleton of a dog (c) and the burial of a young child (e) were found. In the foreground is a slab-lined hearth (d), containing small stones which were heated and dropped into cooking vessels to boil water.

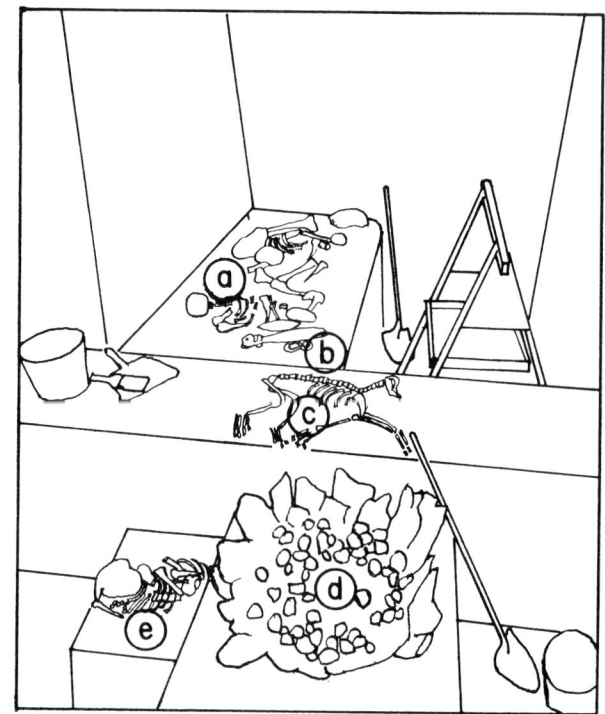

Plate 13. Using the National Museum of Man's reconstruction of a completed excavation unit as a stage set, two museum archaeologists demonstrate a field procedure essential to the interpretation of a site's deposits. A grid of string on the walls of an excavation facilitates the measuring and recording of the different soil profiles and the natural and cultural features.

II. interpreting the remains

Plate 14. Self-image of a warrior. This head is a detail of the club illustrated on p. 70

II. Interpreting the Remains

To provide a detailed picture of a long-dead culture, the archaeologist must be able to interpret what he has found at the dig. This process of interpretation, however, involves much more than merely examining what has been dug from the ground. Just as the fossil hunter is able to reconstruct the forms of ancient animals by studying their living relatives, so the archaeologist reconstructs ancient cultures by interpreting what he has excavated in terms of what is known about living peoples. Such ethnographic studies, especially the reports made by the first anthropologists in a particular area, are invaluable to the archaeologist. Historical documents, too – such as the journals of the early explorers, fur traders, or missionaries – help the archaeologist to fill in many details about a prehistoric culture that he otherwise might never know.

Who were the people?

Prince Rupert harbour, on British Columbia's northern coast, is roughly at the geographical centre of 200 miles (321.8 kilometres) of shoreline between the Nass River in the north and Swindle Island to the south. This is the traditional territory of the Tsimshian-speaking people.

The Tsimshian language is placed in a separate linguistic family, for it has no known close relatives. There are three dialects: *Coast Tsimshian,* which is spoken along the entire coastal area and the lower reaches of the river valleys; *Niskae,* spoken by the villagers on the Nass River; and *Gitksan,* by those who live inland along the banks of the upper Skeena River. The Tsimshian of the coast were divided into fifteen tribes, ten of which had a number of winter villages around Prince Rupert harbour.

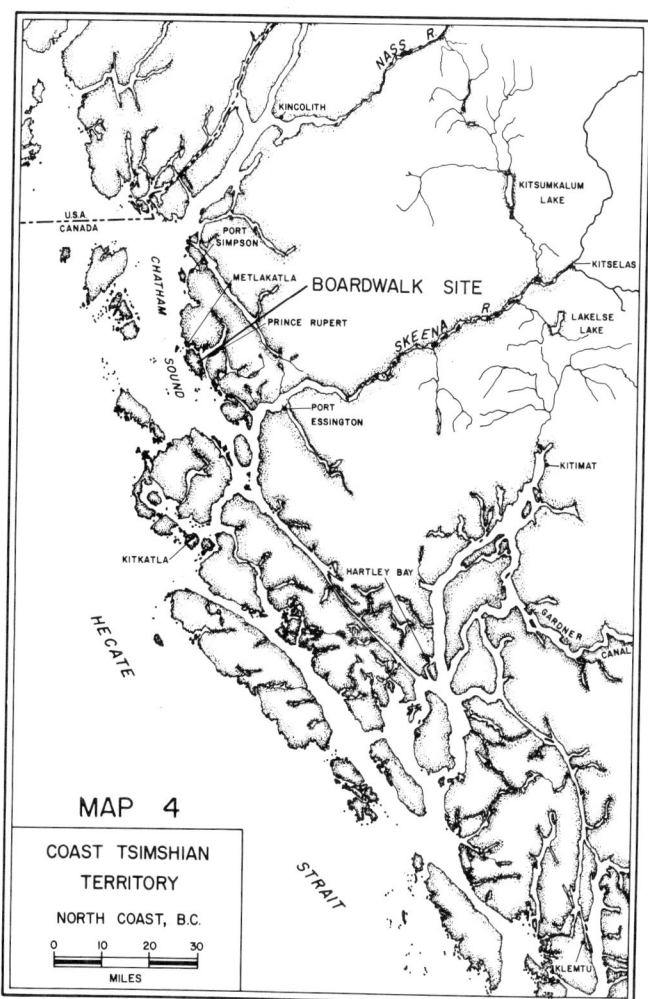

MAP 4
COAST TSIMSHIAN TERRITORY
NORTH COAST, B.C.

Traditional accounts of the Tsimshian people extend their claim to the region far back into the prehistoric past. These traditions are confirmed by the archaeological record, which indicates that the Tsimshian have occupied Prince Rupert harbour and the surrounding coastline continuously for at least 5,000 years. One Tsimshian story recounts a conflict with their northern neighbours, the Tlingit, which led to the abandonment of the harbour area for a generation or two. However, no direct archaeological evidence of this event has been found. The differences between prehistoric Tsimshian artifacts and structures and those of their neighbours are quite clear, and the artifacts found at the harbour villages do not indicate that any other group of people ever lived there.

What the skeletons show

From scientific analysis of skeletal remains, archaeologists learn a great deal about the physical stature of a prehistoric people and the quality of life in a prehistoric village. The Prince Rupert skeletons – over 200 of them – were painstakingly measured and catalogued, and then subjected to rigorous laboratory examination by a physical anthropologist. This highly-skilled researcher compares the bones to each other and to those of other prehistoric populations, to

interpreting the remains

learn what morphological changes may have occurred over time, either by local evolutionary processes or by contacts with other groups of people. Studies of pathology reveal the medical practices and health problems of the villagers.

The Prince Rupert skeletons show that the people were short and stocky. Average adult males were five feet, four inches (1.6 metres) tall, while females were about three inches (7.6 centimetres) shorter. Muscle attachments on the bones were generally more strongly developed in the men than in the women, but adults of both sexes had well developed *humeri* (upper arm bones), which suggests that everyone may have had to paddle canoes.

Infant mortality was high, and difficulties in childbearing shortened the average life span of the women. The mean age of death was in the early thirties, with the men outliving the women by two to three years. Few persons lived past 50 years of age.

Of the diseases that affected the Prince Rupert people, arthritis appears to have been the most common among the adults. Arthritis is a degenerative joint disease which often reflects stresses to which the bone joints are subjected. Among Prince Rupert villagers, the lower back region, the elbow and wrist, and the shoulder ball joints were most severely affected. Several cases of infections and bone tumors, and two cases of spinal curvature, were also noted.

A number of skeletons showed healed fractures, particularly in collar bones and forearms. Such injuries may have occurred when the arms were used to protect the head from violent blows. The head was the second most common area of injury, with depressed fractures occurring on skulls, and a variety of fractures on some faces.

The agonies of certain dental problems were evidently familiar to the villagers. Chewing surfaces of teeth were usually worn down due to an abrasive diet of dried foods, shellfish, roots, and bark. Rapid tooth wear, beginning at an early age, protects against cavity formation by eliminating the pits and fissures in teeth, traps for food particles and bacteria. The extreme wear, however, in many cases resulted in the complete disintegration of tooth crowns and encouraged infection. This led to jaw abscesses. Nearly 50 percent of the adult population had such abscesses, and several individuals were found who had lost teeth because of them.

interpreting the remains

Plate 15. Almost 1,000 years ago, this Tsimshian woman was buried in a box behind her house at the Boardwalk village. Although no traces of the burial box remain, the flexed position is indicative of such burial practice.

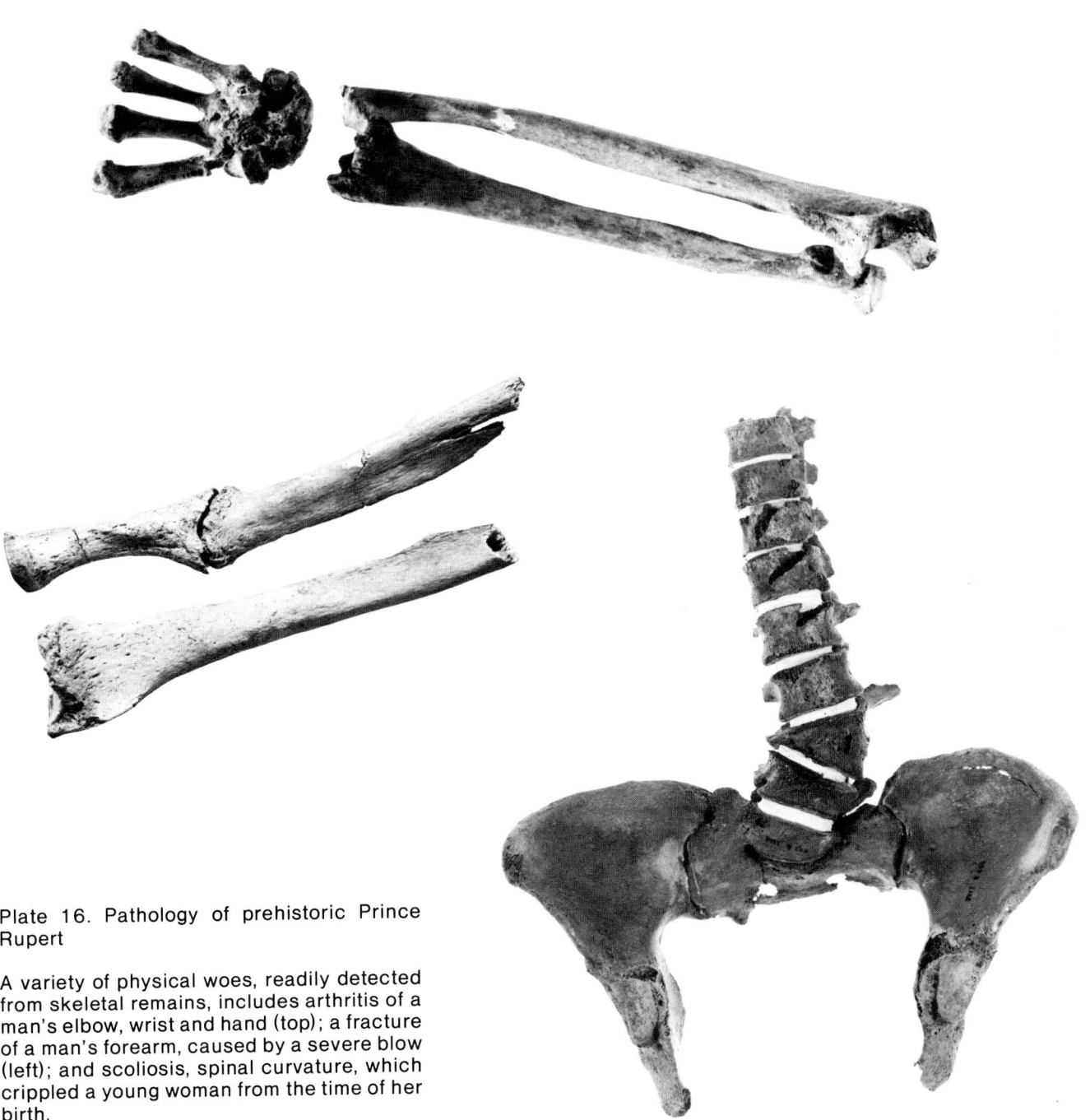

Plate 16. Pathology of prehistoric Prince Rupert

A variety of physical woes, readily detected from skeletal remains, includes arthritis of a man's elbow, wrist and hand (top); a fracture of a man's forearm, caused by a severe blow (left); and scoliosis, spinal curvature, which crippled a young woman from the time of her birth.

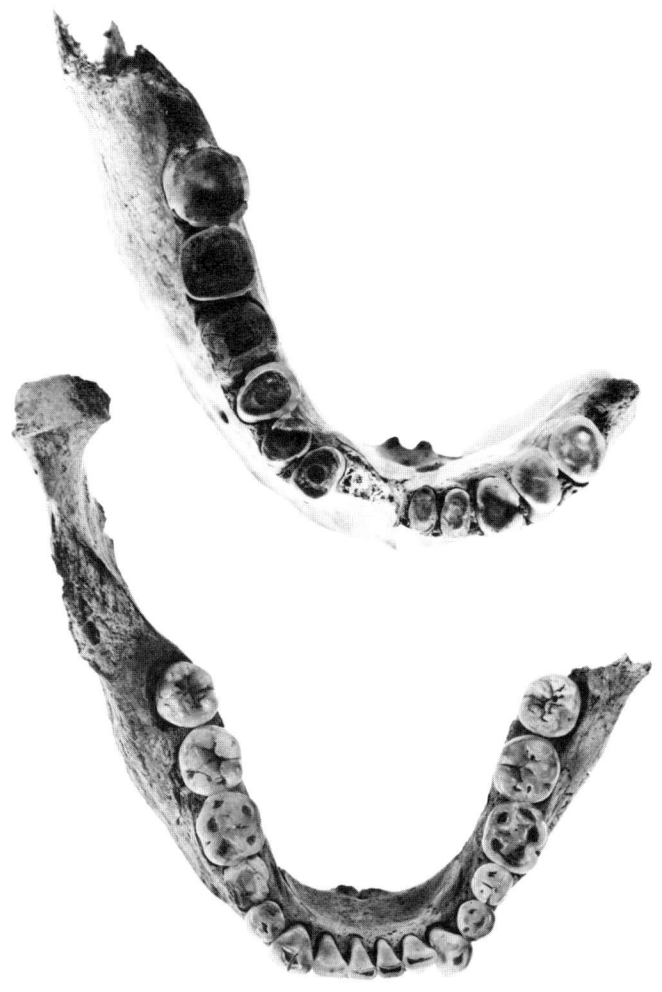

Plate 17. The lower jaws of two Boardwalk villagers show tooth wear which resulted from a diet of coarse foods and the practice of using teeth as tools. Basketry fibres were held in the teeth and softened by saliva, and hides were chewed to make them more pliable. Slight wear is apparent even in the teeth of a 19-year-old man (bottom), while those of a 45-year-old woman (top) are so worn that the pulp cavities are exposed.

Unique tooth wear patterns in several skulls provide information about certain crafts and personal adornments in prehistoric Prince Rupert harbour. Women were skilled in the art of basket-making, and they used their teeth in the work. The tell-tale evidence is seen in the grooves in the grinding surfaces of the front teeth. Grooves were formed by pulling pieces of root fibre or cedar bark between one's teeth in order to prepare fine strands for the weaving of baskets. Teeth were also used to hold a piece of fibre taut, while one end was being worked with the hands.

Another sort of tooth wear resulted from wearing *labrets* (plugs) in one's lower lip. When these were of stone, the lower front teeth were worn flat by the abrading action of the labret against the teeth. Early European explorers to the Northwest Coast reported that only women wore labrets, but the skeletal evidence from Prince Rupert shows that both men and women wore them in prehistoric times.

Analysis of the skeletal remains from the Prince Rupert digs indicates that a single population inhabited the area through the span of time represented from the earliest to the most recent levels. Also, very few physical traits distinguish the Prince Rupert people from other coastal groups in British Columbia. There are similarities, particularly, between villagers at Prince Rupert and the early historic peoples living along the coast further south, suggesting that contacts and marriages were frequent.

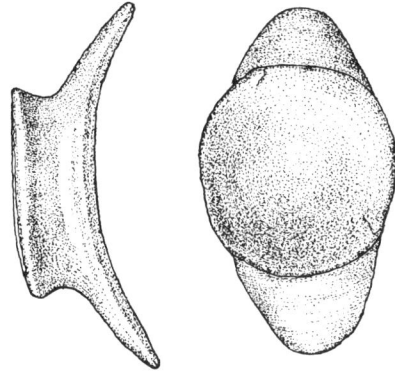

Figure 2. Labret (two views)

Plate 18. Poked through a hole in the lower lip, a labret of wood, stone or bone was a mark of beauty and status among women of the north coast in historic as well as prehistoric times. The practice had nearly died out by the end of the last century. A Haida woman from the Queen Charlotte Islands was still wearing a labret when she was photographed by Richard Maynard in 1884.

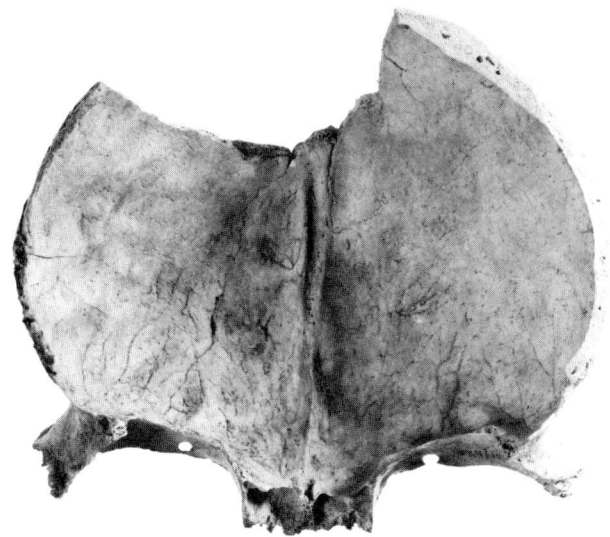

Plate 19. Human bones are occasionally found that show signs of having been deliberately cut in order to produce an artifact. The frontal portion of the skull at the left was partially severed, and may have been intended for use as a small bowl, such as the one above.

interpreting the remains

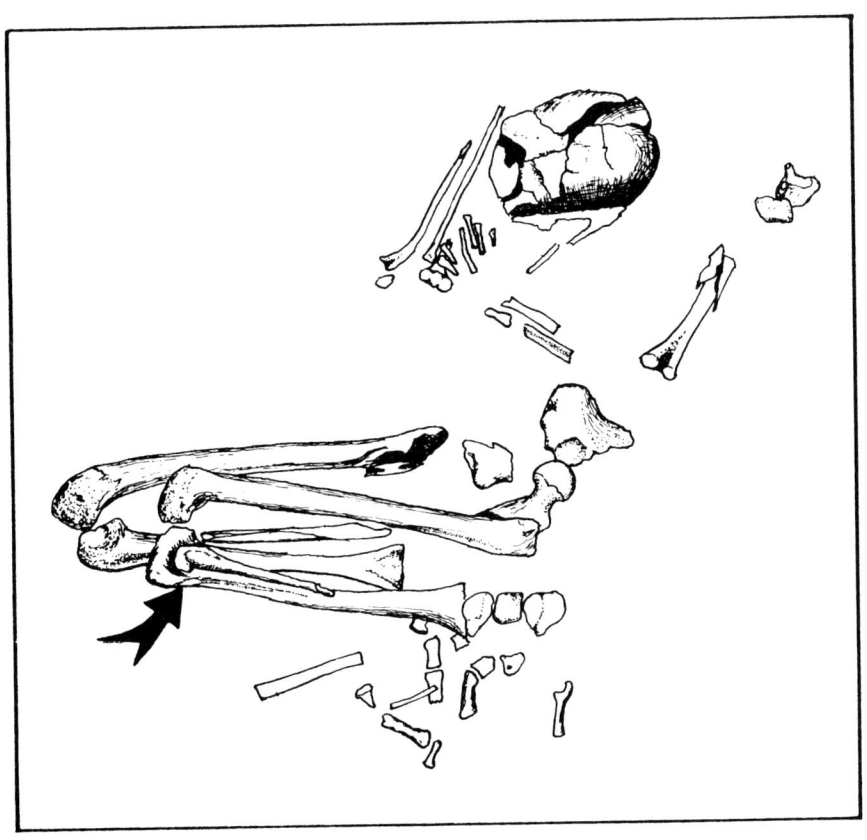

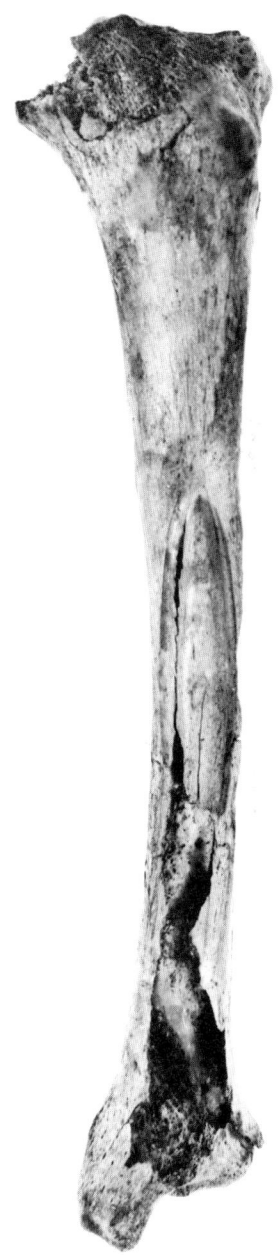

Plate 20. A tibia (shin bone), still attached to the rest of the leg when found, shows a point in the process of being carved from it. The function of such pieces is not known, but they may have served as charms, or some other ritualistic purpose.

interpreting the remains

What did they eat?

The question of what prehistoric peoples ate is one the archaeologist is often well prepared to answer. A large majority of the artifacts found at a typical prehistoric settlement will likely be those used in food gathering, or processing activities. Furthermore, a wide variety of food remains can be preserved in the archaeological record. In the Prince Rupert harbour area, the remains of shellfish, fish, mammals, birds, and vegetable matter have been recovered. Since the Boardwalk site was a winter village, however, only one portion of the annual economic cycle of the Coast Tsimshian is represented here.

Shellfish were very important throughout the 5,000-year span of occupation. The earliest levels almost exclusively contain shellfish varieties, which were readily gathered from the surface of tidal

Plate 21. Clams, dug from the mud flats at low tide, were a village staple in winter, and their shells make up the bulk of the Prince Rupert middens.

Plate 22. Chitons, another mollusk, were common in certain localities, and were easily pried from exposed rocks with sharpened sticks. They were either boiled, roasted in an open fire, or eaten raw. Photographed by Edward S. Curtis in 1915.

interpreting the remains 43

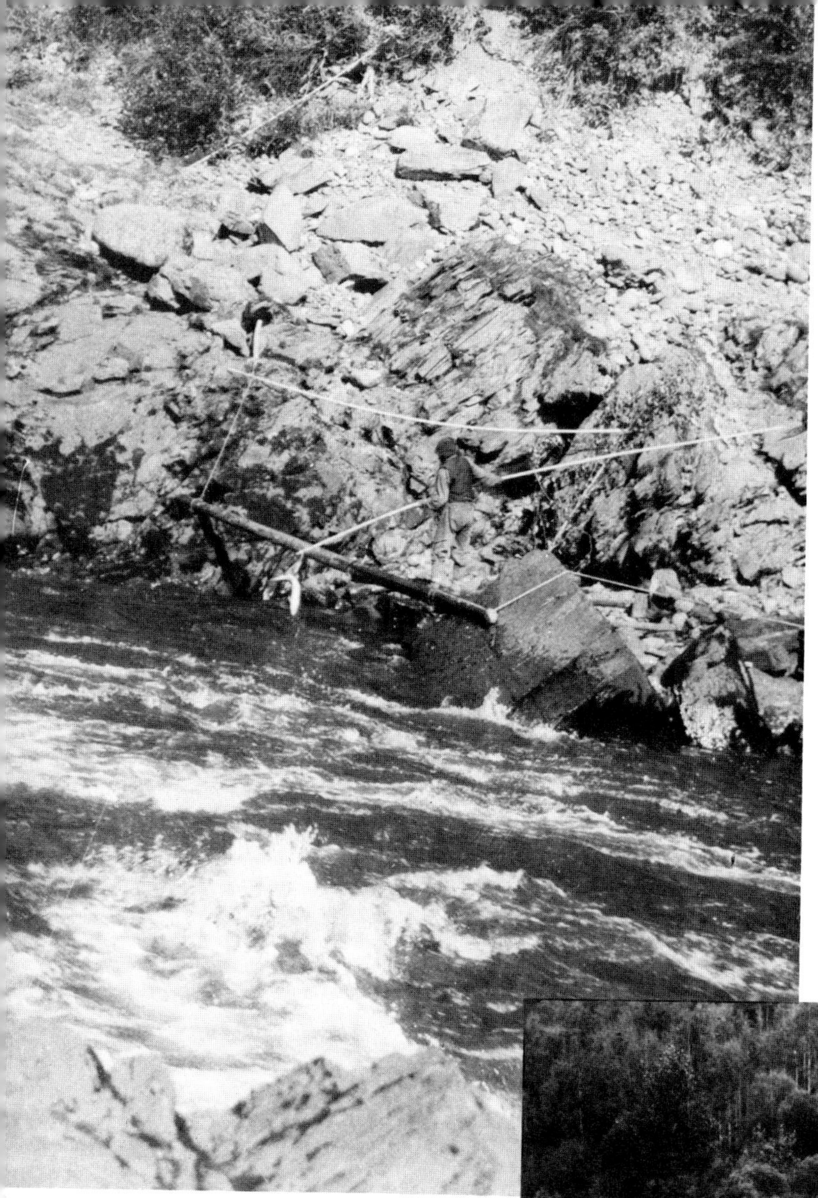

Plates 23 and 24. River fishing

Salmon fishing was a major economic activity of the Tsimshian and other peoples along the Northwest Coast. Fish migrating to spawn were speared from platforms built out over the river (left), or blocked by weirs where they could be speared or caught in basketry traps (below). In shallow slow-moving streams, fish were driven into areas enclosed by walls of piled rocks.

L. Shotridge, 1918

M. Barbeau, 1920

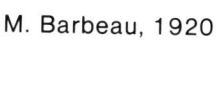

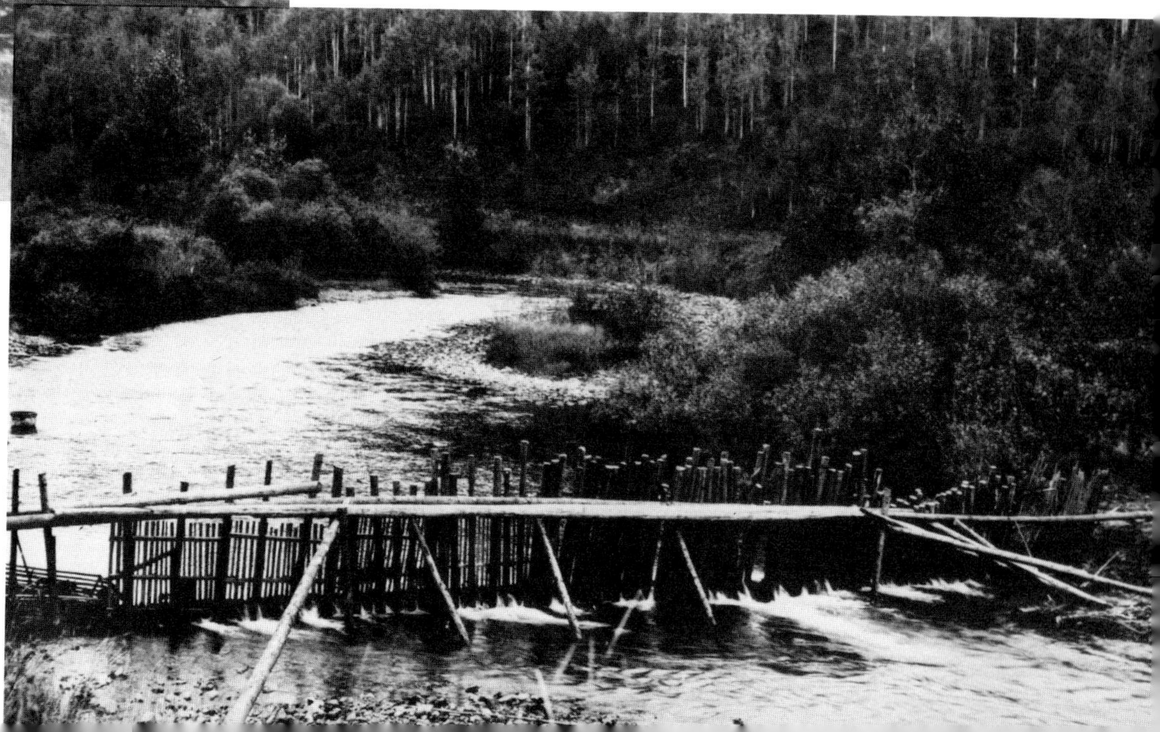

Plates 25 and 26. Sea fishing

Eddies along the rock coastline were ideal places for a fisherman to stand poised to spear salmon. Coastal fishing also included the use of gill nets and trolling from canoes. Bone-pointed wooden hooks weighted with stone sinkers were baited and strung from floats to catch bottom-feeding fish, such as halibut. Photographed by Edward S. Curtis, 1915.

interpreting the remains

flats, rocks, and seaweed beds exposed at low tide. These include mussels and barnacles. In time, the villagers sought a greater range of species, which they dug from the clam beds. Butter and littleneck clams were most commonly harvested, followed by basket cockles and horse clams.

Interpretations, based on historical evidence, suggest that before low tide each day the women assembled their collecting equipment, including digging sticks, open-work baskets, and bone knives for prying shellfish off the rocks. Then they would follow the out-going tide, working in family groups, digging up the shellfish amidst an exchange of village gossip. Extra low tides, which occur once a month, produced a real bonanza for the gatherers.

Clams were steamed in large pits, the meat removed and sun-dried or smoked, and then stored in large cedar bentwood boxes for meals at a later time. To vary the menu, crabs, sea urchins, chitons and sea cucumbers, were gathered from the mud flats and shallow waters.

Another staple of the winter diet was salmon, processed at summer camps along the Skeena River. Five varieties of salmon – sockeye, chum, pink, coho and chinook – were caught by the thousands by household groups. Weirs, basketry traps, barbed harpoons and *leisters* (a kind of barbed spear), were used to catch the fish. The salmon were filleted and smoked or sun-dried, to be stored in boxes for use during the winter months. Along the coast in the spring and fall, the people trolled for salmon.

Halibut, cod and a dozen other species of fish were readily available throughout the year. They were caught by setting lines with baited hooks made of wood and bone, or by jigging. A short but productive spring fishing at the mouth of the Nass River provided a supply of eulachon (candle fish). This fish was dried or rendered to grease by boiling in large plank vats. The grease was the universal condiment in the region, applied to everything from boiled seaweed to salmonberries.

Plates 27 and 28. Nass River eulachon fishery

The fish were strung on racks to dry in the sun (below) or boiled in wooden vats, and the resulting grease skimmed off and stored (above). The Tsimshian carried on a lucrative trade in eulachon grease with their neighbours, the Haida and Tlingit. This activity survives on the Nass River to this day.

interpreting the remains

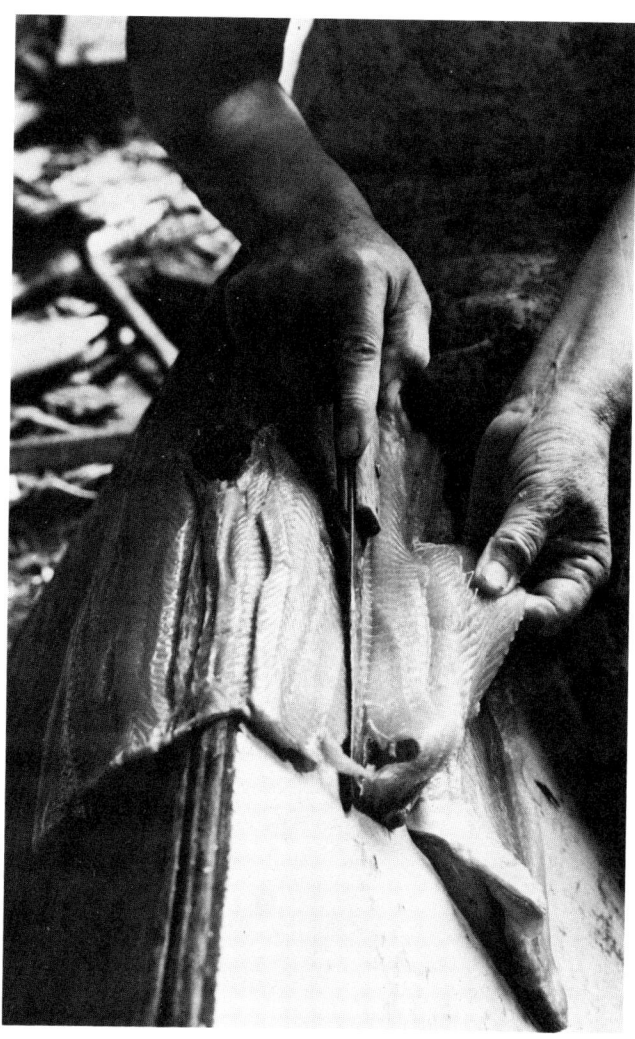

Plate 29. Salmon were cut into thin strips and hung on racks in the smokehouse, a practice still common in Northwest Coast villages today. Port Simpson, 1972.

The annual cycle of the coastal villagers' lives revolved around the procurement of the dietary staple of fish. Considerable energy was expended to acquire the estimated 5 to 10 tons required yearly by each family.

It is surprising, therefore, that fish bones do not make up a large portion of the remains at the Boardwalk site. Several factors may account for this lack. Most fish were filleted and dried at the summer camps, away from the winter village sites. Only the flesh was transported back. It is also probable that special precautions were taken not to offend the fish spirits by tossing the fish bones on the garbage dumps. Returning the fish skeletons to the water from whence they came was a practice noted among the Tsimshian in historic times. If it were not for the numerous bone fishhook barbs at the Boardwalk site, the archaeologist might well have underestimated the importance of fish in the prehistoric economy.

From the mammal bones found in the village deposits, the food supply obtained by hunting can be quantified. In total, the remains of over 40 different species of land and sea mammals have been recognized. Of the land mammals, deer were by far the most important food source, to judge from the counts of archaeological samples. Remains of other animals included dog, porcupine, beaver, bear, muskrat, river otter, mountain goat, and marten. Sea otter was the most heavily hunted sea mammal, but seal, sea lion, and porpoise were also taken. Whales were not hunted, but the carcasses were salvaged when washed ashore.

Butchering marks on some of the mammalian specimens provide evidence of the ways the meat was divided up, and of which cuts were preferred. Charred or calcined bones are rare in the Boardwalk deposits, suggesting that food was not often prepared over an open fire but in cooking boxes.

More than 50 kinds of birds were taken, both for food and for their plumage. Bones of sea ducks, particularly scaups and scoters, and of loons were most common. Eagle, gull, raven, and Canada goose bones have been found in moderate numbers. Bald eagle bones were favoured for making artifacts such as drinking tubes, whistles and beads.

The Boardwalk site yielded little preserved vegetable matter; however, small cedar bark baskets, typical of berry-collecting containers, were found in a water-logged deposit at the Lachane site. One of these baskets had elder-

Plate 30. A 36-foot (10.9-metre) finback whale skeleton, found on an isolated beach, becomes part of the project's faunal collection. To identify thousands of animal bone fragments from a prehistoric site, it is necessary to have comparative samples of all the animals inhabiting the region today.

interpreting the remains 49

Plate 31. One of the most arduous tasks for women in the Northwest Coast economy was digging for roots. Similar collecting baskets and digging sticks were found at one site in the Prince Rupert area. Edward S. Curtis photograph, 1915.

berry seeds in it. Other berries plentiful in the area are salmonberries, huckleberries, bilberries, blueberries, and salal berries. Digging sticks are evidence that roots were gathered. In historic times, coastal peoples gathered the roots of cow parsnip, skunk cabbage, and fern. Seaweed, collected during spring low tides, was perhaps the most important vegetable component of the Boardwalk villagers' diet. It was sun-dried in cakes and stored until used, when it was finely chopped.

In summary, the Coast Tsimshian took advantage of a wide variety of food items. They lived in a bountiful environment, and were aware of its richness and diversity. The ability not only to harvest the abundant seasonal resources, but to preserve them over long periods for later consumption, was an important achievement in the development of the Northwest Coast cultural pattern.

interpreting the remains

A tool for every purpose

Tools, weapons, and other equipment made and used by the Coast Tsimshian people for nearly 5,000 years provide us with an enormous amount of information and understanding of many aspects of their daily lives. To show this, the artifacts on display in the National Museum of Man gallery are arranged according to their uses – hunting or fishing implements, woodworking tools, tools ordinarily used by men or women exclusively, and ornaments and objects of art.

Fishing, as a dominant activity of the Coast Tsimshian, required many different kinds of specialized implements and gear. Bone barbs for catching halibut and codfish are common throughout the deposit. Small bone points, in the shape of an ordinary nail, were embedded in the ends of long wooden rakes to impale herring or eulachon. Stone sinkers, both large and small, used as weights for set lines, gill nets and trolling gear, have been found in quantity. The nets and set lines were buoyed with floats of carved wood. Strands of dried and braided kelp, and sometimes thick cedar bark rope, were used for making lines. The salmon trapped in the weirs built across rivers, were speared with a leister, armed with bone prongs, or with detachable bone harpoon heads.

interpreting the remains

Plate 32. Fishing utensils

A variety of artifacts associated with different stages of the fishing industry are found at Northwest Coast sites. In making nets, a net gauge (a) was used to ensure uniformity of mesh size. Stone sinkers (b and c) helped keep suspended nets in proper position in the water. Hooks, large and small (page 45), were fitted with bone points (d and e). Items needed for cleaning and filleting fish included: a knife (f) made from a deer ulna (one of the foreleg bones), a knife made from a large stone flake (h), and a bone handle (g) into which was set a cutting blade of ground slate.

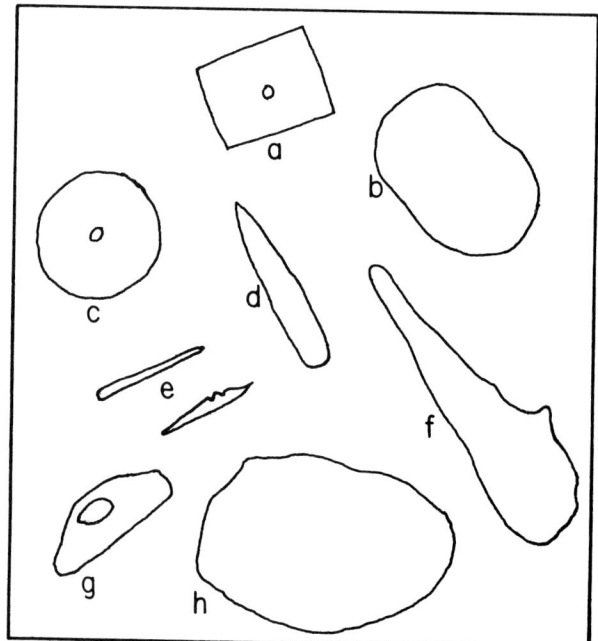

52 *interpreting the remains*

Since roughly 95 percent of the tools and utensils of the Northwest Coast cultures were made of wood, it is not surprising to find a wide range of tools for woodworking. Heavy tools were needed for felling trees and making house planks, canoes, large food containers and storage boxes. Stone splitting adzes, hammerstones and mauls were used, along with wedges of bone and wood, to fell and split cedar logs. Shell and stone adze blades, hafted onto a handle, were used to thin and shape the wood, leaving a characteristic rippled appearance. Final finishing was often accomplished with small chisels and adzes, some made from beaver or porcupine teeth. Abrasive stones were used for smoothing planks that were to be painted.

Identification of the wood species recovered from the waterlogged deposits has revealed that the villagers had a wide knowledge of the properties of various trees. Twelve different kinds of trees were utilized in the manufacture of artifacts. In order of most common occurrence, they include red cedar, western fir, hemlock, yellow cedar, yew, spruce, birch, juniper, alder, pine, maple and crabapple.

Plate 33. In the 1880s, the men of Metlakatla used metal adzes to put the finishing touches on a large canoe hollowed out of a single log. Red cedar, straight-grained and easy to work, was most often used. In earlier times, logs were split with heavy stone adzes (upper left); wedges or chisels were pounded with stone mauls (upper right).

interpreting the remains 55

Plate 34. Light woodworking tools

Besides large splitting adzes and heavy stone mauls (page 55), numerous other implements were required for the construction of houses, canoes, and a great variety of smaller items of wood. Wedges of wood (a) and sea mammal bone (c) were used as well as small adze blades of various materials: chipped stone (b), shell (d), and ground stone (f). The carved antler handle of a graving tool (e) has an inset beaver-incisor cutting edge.

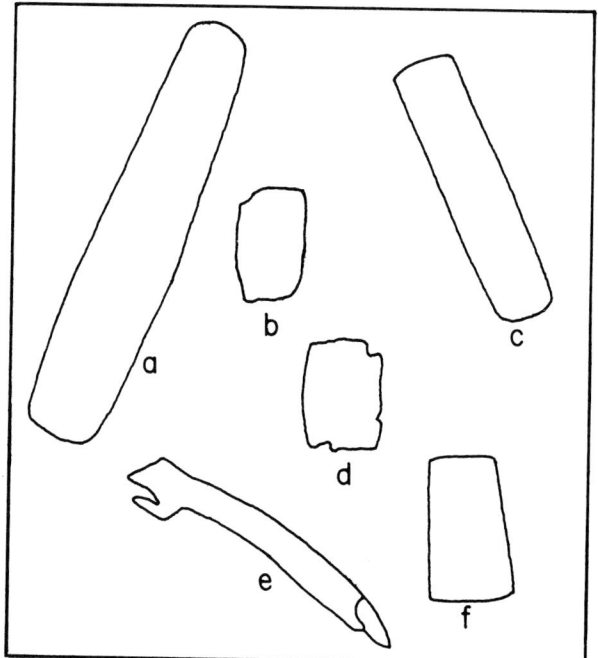

56 *interpreting the remains*

interpreting the remains 57

Besides fishing and woodworking, men's tasks included the hunting of game. Various types of hunting implements were found throughout the deposit. Bows and arrows, tipped with bone, chipped stone, ground stone, or shell points, brought down large land mammals, while sea mammals were stalked with harpoons armed with barbed detachable bone points. The harpooned sea animals, such as seals or sea otters, were killed by the hunters wielding heavy bone or stone clubs.

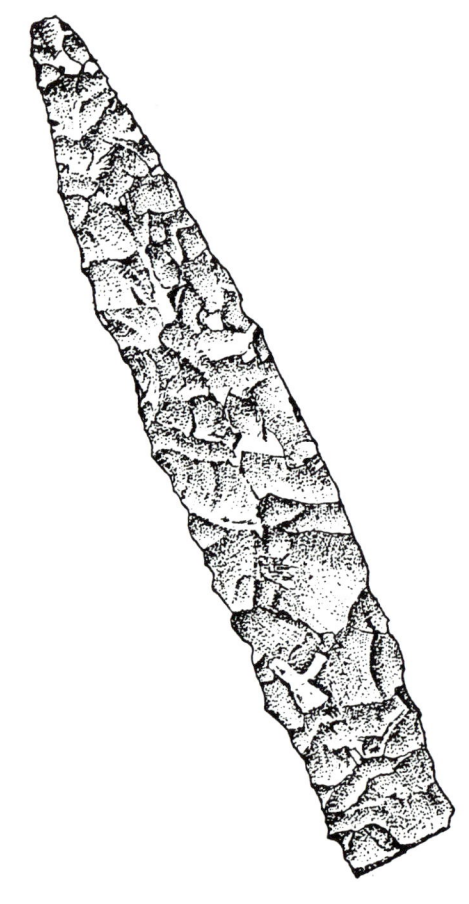

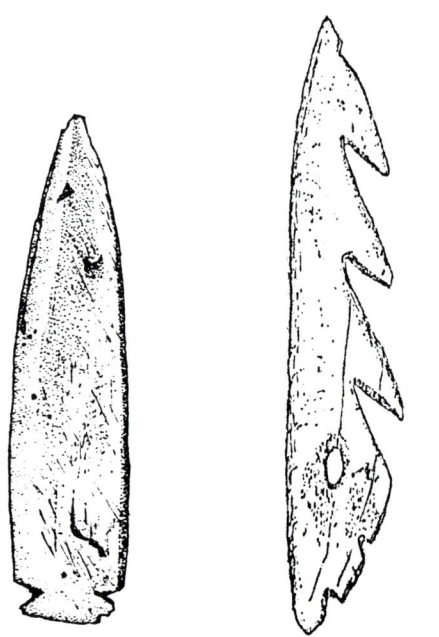

Figure 3. A variety of points used in hunting: ground slate for an arrow (left); chipped basalt for an arrow or lance (upper right); and a bone harpoon point for killing sea mammals. All actual size.

interpreting the remains

Women's work included the weaving of baskets, mats, cordage, nets and clothing. The raw materials for weaving were made into fibres with bark peelers, bark beaters and shredders. Bone awls, needles and spacers were used in making nets and many other kinds of cedar bark articles. Hides were cleaned with scrapers of bone or stone.

The gathering of much of the food other than game and the preparation of it for immediate consumption or storage were important tasks for women. Various types of containers were used in this work, as well as numerous kinds of bone or stone knives and scrapers.

Plate 35. Cedar storage boxes, containing dried salmon and other foods for winter consumption, were covered and stacked indoors. A single board, steamed and slowly bent, forms the sides. Elaborate crest designs were used only on boxes belonging to persons of wealth and high rank.

interpreting the remains

Plate 36. Although a small-scale revival of cedar-bark basket making has taken place in recent years, Mrs. Dorothy Brown of Kitkatla is the last Tsimshian-speaking woman who has practiced the traditional craft all her life. Kitkatla, 1972.

Plate 37. Women's tools

To soften bark for weaving, women in prehistoric times used a bone bark-shredder (a). A spindle whorl (b) was used to spin mountain goat wool for ceremonial blankets. Sewing hides required bone awls (c and d) and needles (e). The large bone awl (f) is made from a deer ulna (one of the foreleg bones).

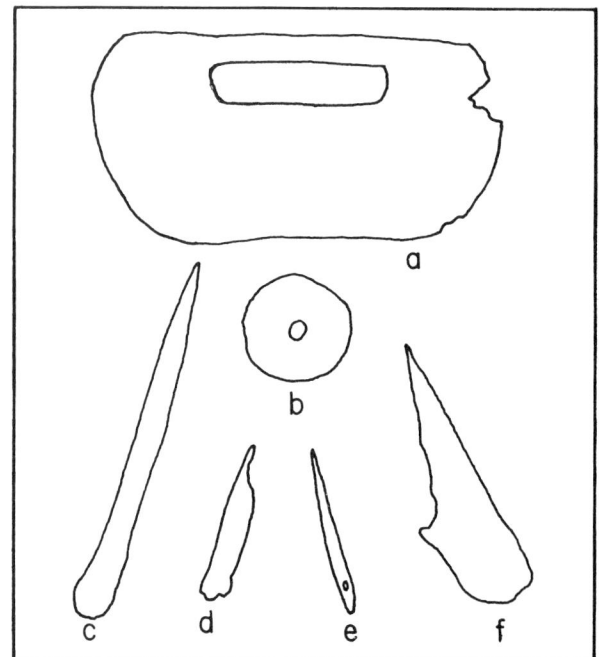

interpreting the remains

Personal adornment and artistic expression

> ...the voyagers who have frequented the different parts of the Northwest Coast often saw there works of painting and sculpture... the execution of which bespoke a taste and perfection which we do not expect to find in countries where the men still seem to have the appearance of savages. But what must astonish most... is to see painting everywhere, everywhere sculpture, among a nation of hunters.*

So wrote Etienne Marchand who, in 1791, was one of the first Europeans to explore the regions along the North Pacific coast. To Marchand, such magnificent art among a people considered in other ways "primitive" presented a paradox. Such attitudes delayed the recognition of the sophisticated nature of the art style until the present day.

From recent archaeological work, however, a detailed history or artistic refinement, from early times to the classic Northwest Coast style, is emerging. Evidence from Prince Rupert, in particular, shows that indigenous art forms developed over a long period of time.

In general, two style concepts can be inferred from the artifacts. (1) *Geometric motifs* involved zoned cross-hatching,

---

*Gunther, Erna. *Indian Life on the Northwest Coast of North America.* University of Chicago Press, 1972, p. 130.

Plate 38. Emblazoned with designs in red ochre and charcoal, the house of Chief Alfred Sgagweit was one of the last traditional dwellings to stand in Fort Simpson. The house front design is a gi'balk, a crest which combines the attributes of two or more animals. A beaver carved on the pole is one of the two crests of the eagle clan to which Chief Sgagweit belonged. This house was destroyed in the 1880s, and a modern house erected in its place. O. C. Hastings photograph, 1879.

interpreting the remains

Colour Plate III. Art Pieces

Craftsmen of prehistoric Prince Rupert applied animal-inspired motifs to a wide variety of utilitarian and decorative objects. Bird figures were often used, and might be incorporated into the design of an antler club (a) or a small stone pendant (h). A tiny bird carved from a mammal canine tooth wears a copper neck ring (c). The fragment of a slate mirror (e) bears an incised human figure, while a wolf forms the handle of a bone comb (g). Other items of personal adornment, such as bone or antler pendants (b,d,f), are common archaeological finds. The objects illustrated here represent 2,000 years of Prince Rupert art.

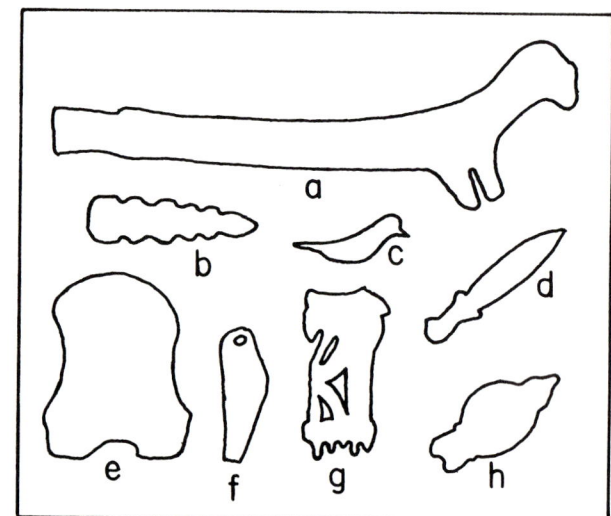

interpreting the remains

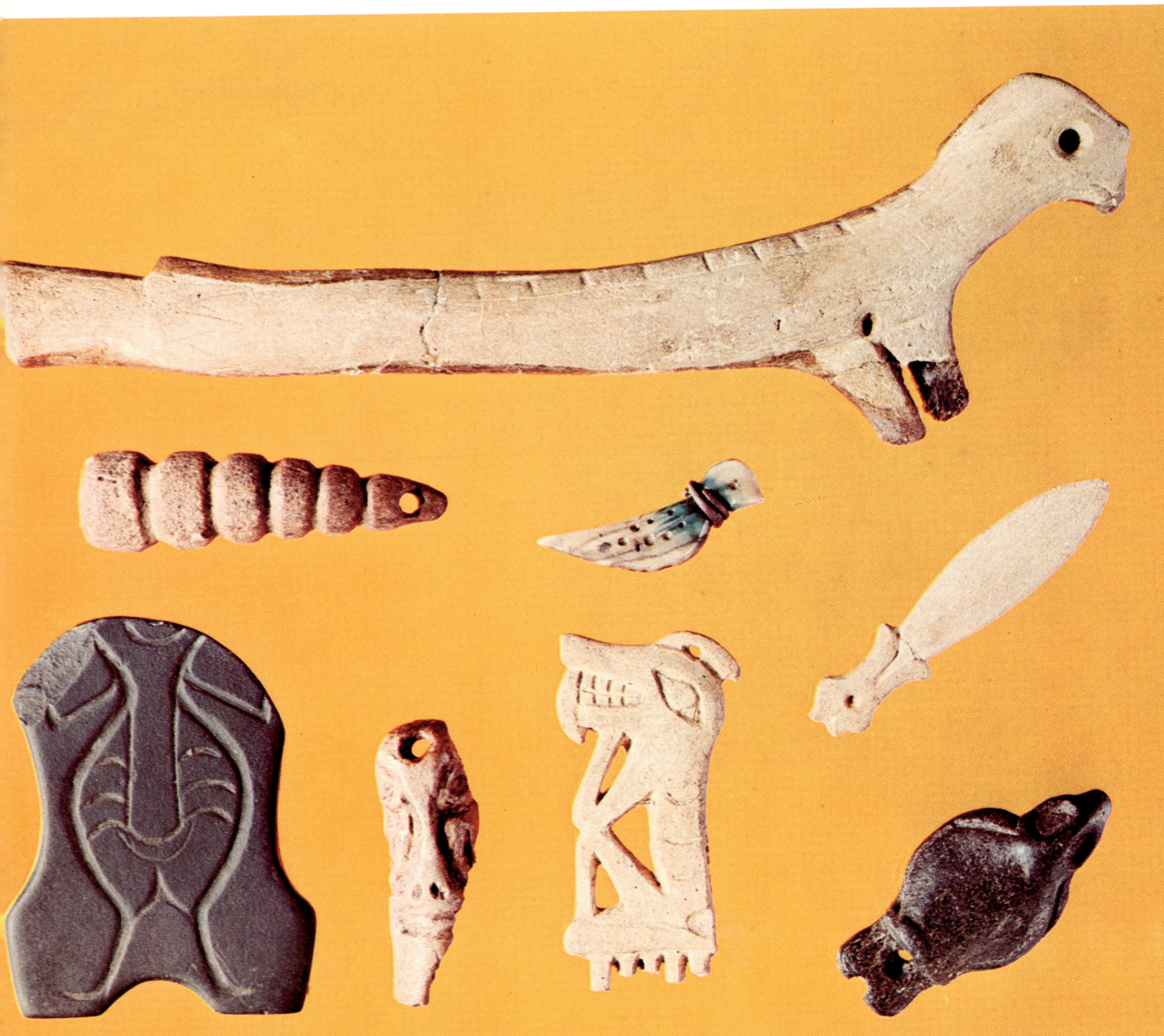

fret designs and nucleated circles. These motifs appear throughout the 5,000-year sequence, and were applied to utilitarian objects such as harpoons or awls, perhaps to signify ownership. (2) *Zoomorphic motifs* are animal forms which were applied to bone and stone objects, starting about 3,000 to 4,000 years ago. Examples include bone handles, bone clubs, stone mauls and adzes.

Items of personal adornment are found throughout the Boardwalk site. There are bone bracelets with incised lines, pendants of bone or stone, labrets, and drilled canine teeth of seals, sea lions, sea otters, bears and other animals, which were suspended from clothing. In the upper levels of the site are found items of wealth, such as beads of dentalium shell, amber and copper, and copper bracelets. These were obtained by trade with people living along other areas of the coast and in the interior.

The artistic endeavours of the Prince Rupert people also can be seen on the rock outcroppings and boulders along the shores. Here numerous petroglyphs of stylized human and animal figures were pecked on the rock faces, as well as occasional designs applied with paint.

Historically, the Tsimshian are regarded as the master painters on the North-

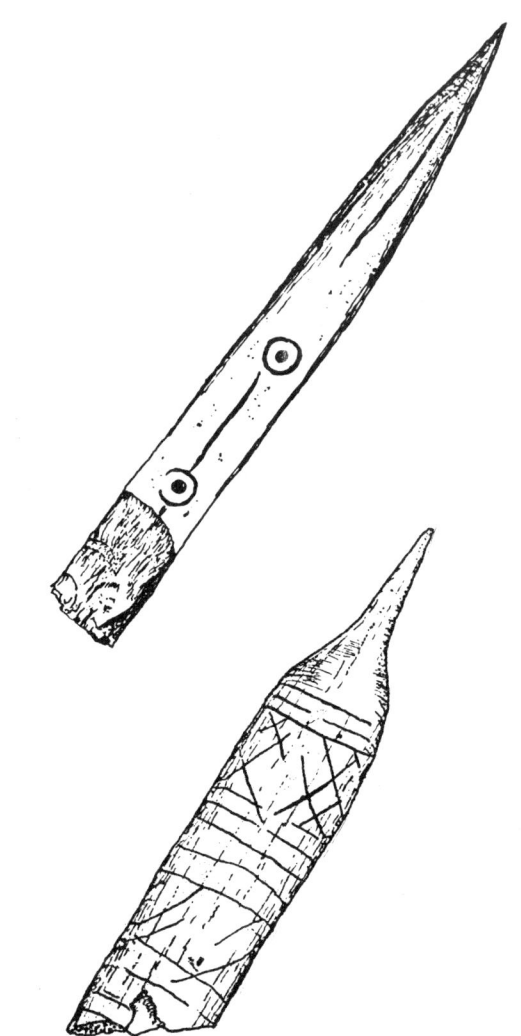

Figure 4. Bone implements with geometric decoration.

66   *interpreting the remains*

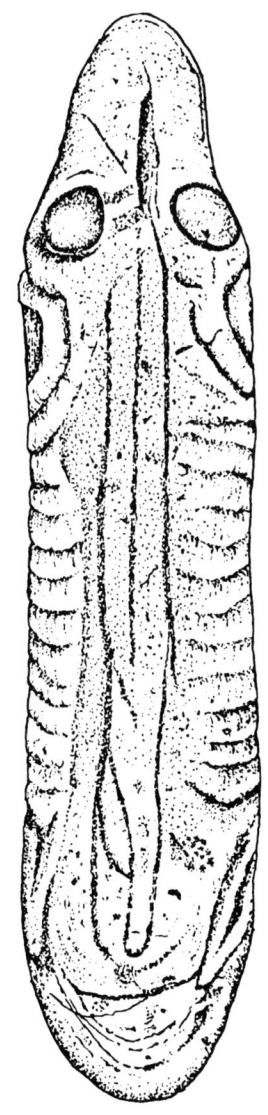

Figure 5. Stone concretion, about 2,000 years old, which has been modified and incised to represent an animal.

west Coast and are famous for their elaborately-painted house fronts, canoes, masks, and storage boxes. Objects of many kinds were no doubt painted in prehistoric times, too, though they are rarely preserved. A wooden harpoon shaft from Prince Rupert has alternating bands of red and black. Pigments recovered from sites include red ochre, charcoal and graphite, and other colours may have been made from a variety of materials, as they were in historic times. These pigments would be mixed with a binder, probably of fish oil. The prehistoric paint kit also included a palette of fine-grained stone and perhaps human-hair paintbrushes, such as are known from ethnographic sources.

Wood, though little of it survives in the archaeological record, undoubtedly provided a major medium for artistic workmanship, whether it was made into items of everyday or ritualistic use. "Totem" poles, which spring to mind in the popular conception of Northwest Coast Indians, are known only from historic villages, such as Kitkatla and Fort (Port) Simpson of the Tsimshian. No remains of them have been found in prehistoric deposits, but their existence can be inferred, in part, from the numerous wood-carving tools found at such sites. Moreover, since "totem" pole carving flourished in historic times, some period

interpreting the remains   67

Plate 39. Rock art

Rock paintings (pictographs) and rock carvings (petroglyphs) serve a number of functions in tribal societies. Images of a face and seven coppers, painted in red ochre on a vertical rock wall (left) were an "advertisement" for a local chief from the Tyee area of the lower Skeena River. Coppers, symbolizing the great wealth and prestige of chief, were large shield-like sheets of copper which were traded over a large portion of the Northwest Coast.

Plate 40. "The Man Who Fell From Heaven"

This petroglyph (right), involves the mythological story of Wegets the Raven, the culture hero of the Tsimshian, and concerns the origin of a line of village chiefs. Born of unions between two mortal brothers and two spirit sisters, Wegets and his brother were expelled from the spirit world. Descending, the brother decided to land on a kelp bed and sank out of sight. Seeing this, Wegets chose to land on the rocks in Prince Rupert harbour, but instead became solidly embedded in a rock at Roberson Point and had to entice the land otter to free him. Wegets subsequently travelled up the Skeena River spreading the arts of mankind, and various rocks upon which he walked or sat are commemorated by the Tsimshian. Photographs by Harlan I. Smith, 1927.

interpreting the remains

– whether short or long – for the development of this cultural pattern must be presumed. These early columns, however, were probably scarce at any of the settlements and, since there were no iron tools, may have been carved in low relief.

The development of sophisticated art styles – as seen in the archaeological evidence – coincides on the Northwest Coast with the first evidence of social ranking and, possibly, with the earliest forms of the *potlatch*. Historically, the potlatch was a social mechanism which, by a ritualized system of public exchange, reinforced a person's or household's claims to economic territory, origin stories, dances, etc. It was the primary institution which bound the society together. It culminated in the elaborate community displays witnessed – and often misinterpreted – by the European visitors to the Northwest Coast.

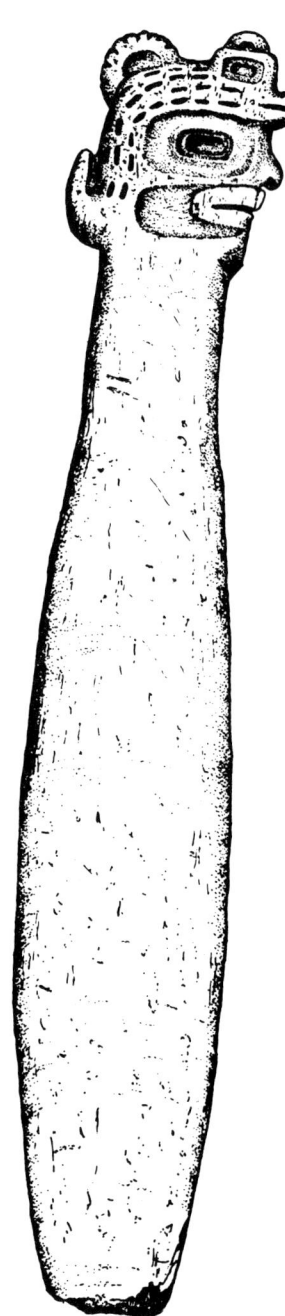

Figure 6. Part of a unique find at the Boardwalk site, this 17-inch-long (43.2 centimetre), whalebone club was unearthed from a cache of warrior's items nearly 1,000 years old. The animal on the headgear probably represents the owner's crest.

III. synthesis of the archaeological interpretation

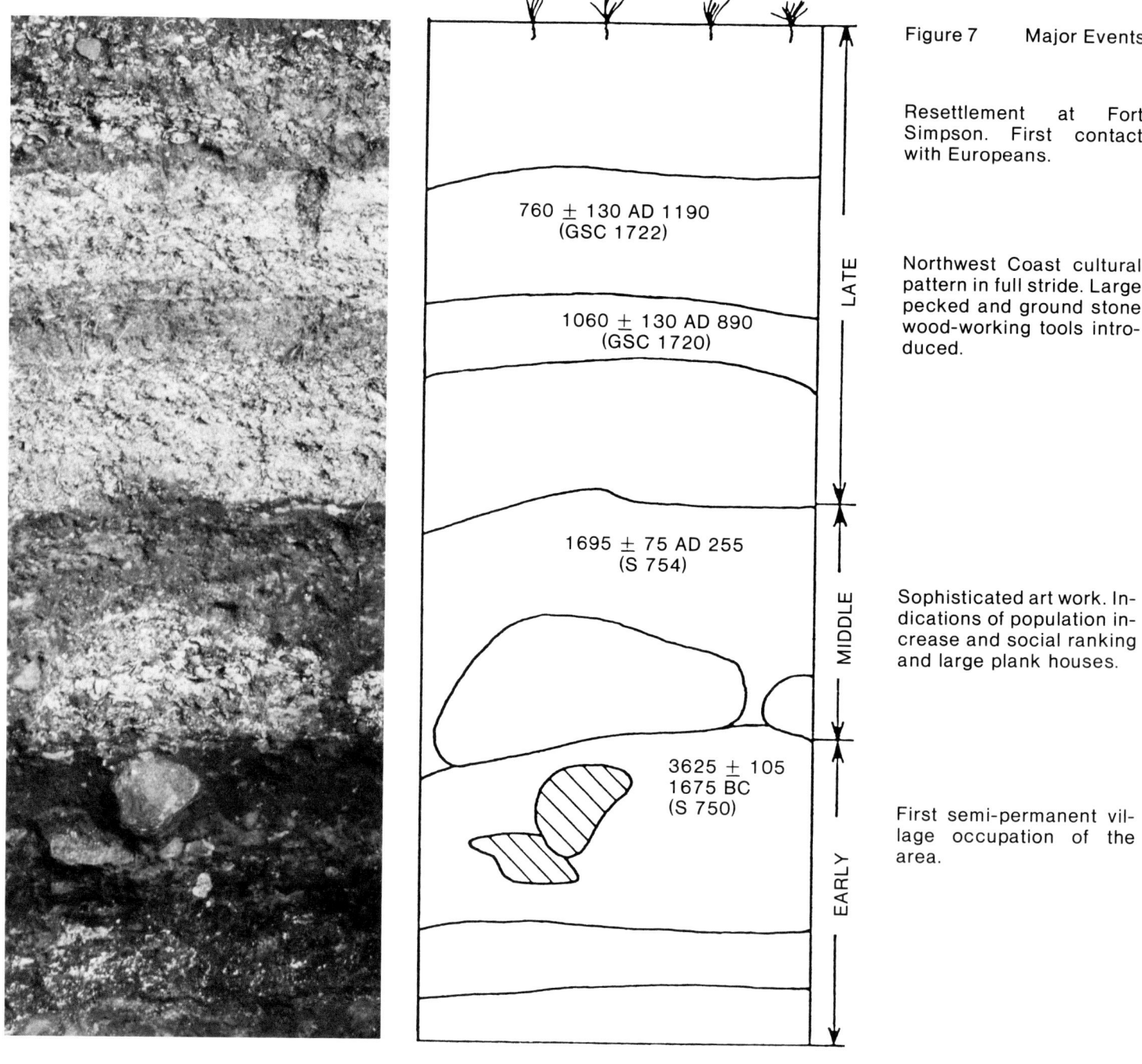

Figure 7   Major Events

III. Synthesis of the Archaeological Interpretation

An Outline of Coast Tsimshian Prehistory

After the excavation has been completed, the artifacts, features and samples analyzed, and their stratigraphic associations and functions interpreted, the archaeologist must provide a synthesis of the history of the site, based on the intrepretations. To do this, a chronological skeleton is set up using the radiocarbon dating method, upon which the archaeologist can reconstruct the flesh of the living culture. The following outline has resulted from the research in the Prince Rupert harbour area.

Early   3000 B.C. to 1500 B.C.
Middle 1500 B.C. to A.D. 500
Late   A.D. 500 to A.D. 1830

A simple chronology of this sort provides convenient divisions of the prehistory of a particular area, which can be used for comparative purposes when looking at the cultural continuum as a whole. A typical archaeological sequence, such as this one for the Prince Rupert area, is seen as a series of developing technological traditions with an accumulative effect through time. New elements are appended to the basic pattern, but they do not significantly alter it. In other words, as more insights into the cultural pattern come to light from the analysis of the artifacts and other remains, they are fitted into the existing chronological framework and increase the archaeologist's understanding of the lives of the people at various stages.

At Prince Rupert, the changes that occur are quantitative and likely reflect elaborations in the social and economic organization, rather than any gross alterations in the basic lifeways of the people. For example, the rapid build-up of the middens during later periods is evidence of rapidly growing population. This population increase necessitated the development of social mechanisms which balanced populations to their environment, in ways which increased the efficiency of their exploitation of the resources available to them. Among the Tsimshian, this process can be seen in growth or rank and privilege.

Early – 3000 B.C. to 1500 B.C.

The early levels of the Prince Rupert middens show that far fewer people lived there 4,000 to 5,000 years ago than at the time of first contact with Europeans. Midden debris accumulated at a slow rate at all village sites. However, the basic economic pattern is established at this time. From spring until fall, the small household groups travelled to temporary camps spread over a large territory to obtain seasonally abundant resources. They then returned to winter in their coastal villages around Prince Rupert harbour.

Few features can be recognized, but indications are that houses were considerably smaller than those of later times. Post molds for house superstructures are only 6 to 8 inches (15 to 20 centimetres) in diameter, and no signs have been found that any portion of the house floors were "sunken", as in later dwellings. No evidence of status differentiation in the house constructions has been found. Even in the earliest period, however, the houses were lined up in orderly fashion, parallel to the beach.

Plates 41 and 42. Ceremonialism

Painted in the mid-1800s by a resident of Fort Simpson, Fred Alexcee, these illustrations provide information about aspects of Tsimshian life that cannot be reconstructed from archaeological data alone. Above, a man in a bear costume displays a copper shield, a symbol of wealth, while performing at a feast. The bear probably was the crest of the chief holding the feast. In a Chief's Dance, right, the host welcomes his guests to the event. As a sign of peace, eagle down was released from the headgear by his movements and sprinkled down upon the guests.

74 *synthesis of the archaeological interpretation*

Plate 43. Warfare

Intergroup hostility was not uncommon in Tsimshian life, as the many bashed skulls found in excavations testify. In raids for slaves, or to avenge a wrong, warriors wielded heavy stone and bone clubs (above). The methods of warfare, however, are difficult to determine in detail from archaeological data alone. A warrior wearing body armour and helmet (right), depicted by a nineteenth-century Tsimshian artist, provides more revealing evidence.

Middle – 1500 B.C. to A.D. 500

About 1500 B.C. a larger population is reflected in rapid midden build-up, larger village sites and the construction of larger houses. Heavy woodworking tools of wood and pecked and ground stone, such as wedges, grooved adzes, hammers, and plank smoothers associated with house building and canoe making, coincide with the appearance of the larger houses.

By this time, village settlement patterns show definite evidences of ranked social structure, with the house of the highest ranking chief standing in the centre of the house row, and the houses of lesser lineage chiefs extending out in both directions in descending order. The houses of village chiefs were larger and more elaborate than the others, often with interior pits cribbed with planks.

Dentalium shells, amber and obsidian are evidence of a developing trade in prestigious items with people in other areas. Encounters with other groups sometimes were hostile to judge from the stone and bone clubs, daggers, trophy human bones, and "bashed" skulls which were recovered. Also appearing at this time is the crest style of zoomorphic art – to advertise the traditions and prerogatives of extended household groups.

Late – A.D. 500 to A.D. 1830

The Northwest Coast cultural pattern is in full stride by A.D. 500, and most of the cultural elements in existence at the time of contact with European explorers can be recognized in the latest levels.

Plate 44. Fred Alexcee drawing

synthesis of the archaeological interpretation **77**

Clear status differentiation is apparent. The social ranks include nobles, commoners and slaves, as reflected in the differences in burial patterns and grave furnishings. Nobles are treated to elaborate grave goods such as weapons for the men (daggers, clubs, slat armour); while the women have shell and amber pendants, shell beads and copper earrings. The lids of some burial chests are inlaid with sea-otter teeth. Commoners have simple burials with no trappings. Slaves or captives, represented by burials of different physical type, are buried in an extended form, without boxes, or are mutilated.

Although rapid build-up of village debris, particularly shellfish remains, was most rapid from this period, the number of house sites appears to have been fixed by tradition. Lineages, or house units, held their individual house sites along with a variety of seasonal resource areas, such as fishing, hunting and collecting grounds, to balance their annual cycle. We may speculate that a new social practice arose for balancing the number of people assigned to each house with the resources claimed by that house. Such practices included population transfers from overpopulated houses, short of resources, to house groups whose resources were less taxed; marriage alliances between houses; successful claims to new resources through potlatching; and occasionally by conquest of resource areas from neighbouring tribes.

During a period of 50 years following the time Europeans first visited the Prince Rupert area in the 1780s, the Tsimshian had sporadic contacts with explorers and fur traders. Trade goods were introduced from these sources, but they had little effect on the overall prehistoric pattern, and the Tsimshian way of life remained relatively unchanged. The trade items found in the deposits are mostly decorative – glass beads, buttons, and sheet copper, locally manufactured into tinklers. Also found are fragments of glazed ceramic, and a few pieces of firearms and gunflints. No iron adzes, chisels or picks have been recovered at Prince Rupert harbour, although traders' journals of the period indicate that such items were traded in quantity to other northern groups at this time.

Plate 45. Fort Simpson in the winter of 1873

Built by the Hudson's Bay Company in 1834, Fort Simpson became the home of the Tsimshian from Prince Rupert harbour. The fort comprised a trade shop, a warehouse, officers' quarters, a mess hall, and houses and shops for Bay Company employees. Two bastions, each with four guns, were situated at opposite corners of an 18-foot-high (5.5 metre) palisade of thick cedar planks. The post was closed in 1911. After 1915, when the last buildings were burned down, the settlement came to be known as Port Simpson. Photograph by C. Horetzky.

Plates 46 and 47. Old Metlakatla in 1881

Two hundred houses, each with its own garden, were built at Metlakatla by the Tsimshian followers of Anglican missionary William Duncan. The success of this social experiment depended on the economic well-being of the community, which had carpenter's and blacksmith's shops, a sawmill, and a salmon cannery. Public buildings included a town hall, a trade hall (large building at far left), a school house, a court house, and a jail. The town also boasted the largest church north of San Francisco and west of the Mississippi at the time. Photographed by E. Dossetter, in 1881.

The Tsimshian Today

In 1834, the Hudson's Bay Company built a fur-trading fort, twenty miles (32 kilometres) to the north of Prince Rupert harbour. Around this time the Tsimshian, about 2,500 in number, abandoned their winter villages around Prince Rupert and resettled in Fort Simpson. By the early 1860s, disease had reduced the population by one third.

In 1862 about 50 people, encouraged by a missionary, William Duncan, left Fort Simpson and moved back to the village of Metlakatla, one of their old village sites in the Prince Rupert area. There Duncan set up a model Christian community, and the population grew to a thousand residents. A second split in the community, resulting from a dispute between Duncan and the Anglican bishop, led the missionary and 800 of his staunchest supporters to move over the border to Alaska in 1887.

By 1905, most of the public buildings at Metlakatla had been destroyed by fire, and the village declined in importance. Today, the population is less than 100.

The major Coast Tsimshian community in British Columbia is Port (Fort) Simpson, a thriving town boasting a modern cannery and a population of 1,100.

The city of Prince Rupert, with a population of over 15,000, offers an urban centre and employment in the fishing and forest products industries. Economic patterns have changed little from the ancient past to recent times, with the sea and the forests still providing the major resources.

synthesis of the archaeological interpretation

Colour Plate IV.
Inspired by the past,
Born in the present,
Bequeathed to the future....

In the years following the earliest European explorations along the Northwest Coast, the encroachment of Whites into Tsimshian lands caused a rapid and severe disintegration of the traditional way of life. Besides many new diseases which reduced the native population, the disrupting influences of missionaries determined to stamp out pagan ways, and the introduction of government authority and institutions left the Tsimshain — like most Indian groups — alienated from their own culture.

Until fairly recently, little has been done to alter this condition or to revive the traditions of the past. Today, however, the Tsimshian people are learning how much was lost, and are striving to regain the values of their former culture. The arts, mythologies, ceremonial life, family life, even the foods of the past, are being relearned. More important, the sense of identity with these traditions is being rekindled.

'Ksan is both the name of a reconstructed Tsimshian village and of an association dedicated to the teaching and preservation of Tsimshian culture. The village, located in Gitksan territory at the junction of the Skeena and Bulkley Rivers, was officially opened in 1970. It features a museum, an active craft school, and a store which retails the artists' work. The highly acclaimed 'Ksan dance group has toured many major cities in Canada and the United States.

The successful blending of traditional values with contemporary viewpoints and the avid participation of the Gitksan people, young and old, ensures the future existence of the project.

acknowledgements

To the people of the north coast of British Columbia we extend our gratitude for their support and interest over the past ten years. We wish to thank in particular the people of the Port Simpson and Metlakatla Bands, whose heritage is the inspiration for this work.

To the more than 120 students who worked on the field crews, many as volunteers; to the students who assisted in the laboratory work in Ottawa, especially Rob Ferguson and Sally Cole; and to Sheila Coulson and her crew of students, who spent three summers constructing "The Dig", we present this work as one end-product of their labours.

To our colleagues, Dr. Jerome Cybulski, who is conducting the osteological research studies, and Frances Stewart, the archaeofaunal analyst, our thanks for their summary outlines included in this guide.

Dave Laverie of our staff, and the National Museums' of Canada Photographic Section are responsible for the excellent illustrations.

Plates 1 and 28 are by courtesy of the Smithsonian Institution, Washington, D.C.; Plates 2 and 27 are by courtesy of the British Columbia Provincial Museum, Victoria, B.C.; Plate 33 is by courtesy of the Museum of Northern British Columbia, Prince Rupert, B.C.; Plates 41, 42 and 44 are by courtesy of the Glenbow-Alberta Institute, Calgary, Alberta; Plate 45 is by courtesy of the Public Archives of Canada, Ottawa. All other illustrations are from the National Museums of Canada, Ottawa.

Final thanks are extended to Mrs. Joyce Hinton and Mrs. Myrtle Scott for typing the manuscript, and to Roy Vontobel for his assistance in preparing the manuscript.

suggested reading list

What is Archaeology? – General

Alimen, H.

1950 *Atlas de Préhistoire.* Vol. 1 Editions. N. Boubée & Cie., Paris.

Borden, Charles E.

1952 *A Uniform Site Designation Scheme for Canada.* Anthropology in British Columbia. No. 3, Victoria, pp. 44-48. Summarized in Oracle, National Museum of Man, National Museums of Canada, No. 7 (en français) and No. 8 (English), 1975.

Deetz, James

1967 *Invitation to Archaeology.* American Museum of Science Books, The Natural History Press.

1971 *Man's Imprint From the Past: Readings in the Methods of Archaeology.* Little, Brown and Company, Boston.

Fagan, Brian M.

1970 *Introductory Readings in Archaeology.* Little, Brown and Company, Boston.

Hester, Thomas R., Robert F. Heizer and John A. Graham

1975 *Field Methods in Archaeology* (6th Edition) Mayfield Publishing Company, Palo Alto, California

Hole, Frank
and Robert F. Heizer

1973 *An Introduction to Prehistoric Archaeology.* (Third Edition). Holt, Rinehart and Winston, Inc., New York.

Laming-Emperaire, A.

    1963 *L'Archéologie Préhistorique.* Le Rayon de la Science, Editions du Seuil, Paris.

Willey, Gordon R.

    1966 *An Introduction to American Archaeology. Volume I. North and Middle America.* Prentice-Hall, Inc., New Jersey.

Wright, James V.

    1976 *Six Chapters of Canada's Prehistory.* National Museum of Man, National Museums of Canada, Ottawa.

Indians in British Columbia – General

Barbeau, Marius

    1950 (1964)
        Totem Poles (2 volumes). National Museum of Canada, Bulletin No. 119, Ottawa.

British Columbia, Department of Education, Division of Curriculum

    1951-53
        British Columbia heritage series: our native peoples. 10 volumes: *V.1. Introduction to Our Native Peoples; V.2. Coast Salish; V.3. Interior Salish; V.4. Haida; V.5. Nootka; V.6. Tsimshian; V.7. Kwakiutl; V.8. Kootenay; V.9. Dene; V.10. Bella Coola.* Victoria.

Drucker, Philip

    1965 *Cultures of the North Pacific Coast.* Chandler Publishing Company, San Francisco.

Duff, Wilson

    1964 *The Indian History of British Columbia: Volume 1, The Impact of the White Man.* Anthropology in British Columbia, Memoir 5, Victoria.

    1975 *Images Stone B.C.: Thirty Centuries of Northwest Coast Indian Sculpture.* Hancock House, Saanichton.

Gunther, Erna

    1972 *Indian Life on the Northwest Coast of North America as Seen by the Early Explorers and Fur Traders During the Last Decades of the Eighteenth Century.* The University of Chicago Press, Chicago.

Hill, Beth and Ray

    1974 *Indian Petroglyphs of the Pacific Northwest.* Hancock House Publishers, Saanichton.

Holm, Bill

    1965 *Northwest Coast Indian Art: An Analysis of Form.* University of Washington Press, Seattle.

Levi-Strauss, Claude

    1975 *La Voie Des Masques (2 tomes).* Skira, Genève, Switzerland.

McFeat, Tom

    1967 (1971)
    Indians of the North Pacific Coast. University of Washington Press, Seattle.

Stewart, Hilary

    1973 *Artifacts of the Northwest Coast Indians.* Hancock House Publishers, Saanichton.

Tsimshian

Adams, John W.

    1973 *The Gitksan Potlatch.* Holt, Rinehart and Winston, Toronto.

Barbeau, Marius

    1929 (1973)
    Totem Poles of the Gitksan, Upper Skeena River, British Columbia. National Museum of Canada, Bulletin No. 61, Anthropological Series, No. 12, Ottawa.

    1961 *Tsimsyan Myths.* National Museum of Canada. Bulletin No. 174, Anthropological Series, No. 12, Ottawa.

Evans, Hubert

    1954 *Mist on the River.* New Canadian Library No. 86, McClelland and Stewart, Toronto.

Garfield, Viola E.
and Paul S. Wingert

    1966 *The Tsimshian Indians and Their Arts.* University of Washington Press, Seattle.

Garner, F. Richard
and George F. MacDonald

    1972 *Haida and Tsimshian: A Photographic History.* National Museum of Man, National Museums of Canada, Ottawa.

Large, R. G.

    1957 *The Skeena – River of Destiny.* Mitchell Press, Vancouver.

MacDonald, George F. et al

    1972 *'Ksan – Breath of Our Grandfathers.* National Museum of Man, National Museums of Canada, Ottawa.

Usher, Jean

    1974 *William Duncan of Metlakatla. A Victorian Missionary in British Columbia.* National Museum of Man, National Museums of Canada, Publications in History, No. 5, Ottawa.